Perfect Strangers?
Deep Purple 1984-1993

Laura Shenton

Perfect Strangers?
Deep Purple 1984-1993

Laura Shenton

WYMER PUBLISHING
Bedford, England

First published in 2023 by Wymer Publishing
Bedford, England www.wymerpublishing.co.uk Tel: 01234 326691
Wymer Publishing is a trading name of Wymer (UK) Ltd

Copyright © 2023 Laura Shenton / Wymer Publishing.

Print edition (fully illustrated): **ISBN: 978-1-915246-28-8**

Edited by Jerry Bloom.

The Author hereby asserts her rights to be identified
as the author of this work in accordance with sections
77 to 78 of the Copyright, Designs & Patents Act 1988.

All rights reserved. No part of this publication may be
reproduced or transmitted in any form or by any means,
electronic or mechanical, including photocopying, or any
information storage and retrieval system, without written
permission from the publisher.

This publication is sold subject to the condition that it shall not,
by way of trade or otherwise, be lent, re-sold, hired out or
otherwise circulated without the publishers' prior consent in any
form of binding or cover other than that in which it is published
and without a similar condition including this condition
being imposed on the subsequent purchaser.

eBook formatting by Coinlea.
Printed and bound in Great Britain by
CMP, Dorset.

A catalogue record for this book is available from the British Library.

Typeset/Design by Andy Bishop / 1016 Sarpsborg
Cover design by 1016 Sarpsborg.

Contents

Preface	7
Listen, Learn, Read On	9
Over The Rainbow	21
Who Do We Think We Are	29
Knocking At Your Back Door	53
Nobody's Home	73
Living Wreck	91
The Battle Rages On…	115
Discography	139
Tour Dates	149

"We live different lives, and we're a diverse bunch of characters. If you decided to put five guys in the band, you wouldn't pick us!"

– Ian Gillan (1988)

Preface

The 1984 reunion of Deep Purple Mk2 (henceforth Mk2.2) is a fascinating one — not just in terms of the music, the live performances and the behind-the-scenes dramas, but in terms of how, amongst fans of the band, this period so drastically divides opinion.

If you say to most fans, Deep Purple Mk2.1 (the first round of the Mk2 line-up of Ian Gillan on vocals, Roger Glover on bass, Ritchie Blackmore on guitar, Jon Lord on organ, and Ian Paice on drums), the general response is one of positivity. Most people, regardless of what they may say about Mk1, Mk3 and Mk4, rarely have any tremendously strong complaints against Mk2.1.

For instance, I don't think, in my years of talking to other Deep Purple fans, I have ever heard anyone say that Mk2.1 was "the worst" line-up. The same can't be said for the other line-ups. However, when the topic of Mk2.2 comes up, it's a different approach entirely. No longer is the overall feeling one of unanimous agreement that this line-up was "good", or "essential", or "the best".

It's fascinating that even though Deep Purple Mk2.2 consists of the same pool of talent responsible for *In Rock*, *Fireball*, *Machine Head* and *Who Do We Think We Are*, not all fans of the band look favourably upon their 1984 reunion.

In this book, as well as providing lots of facts and insight, I will delve into the opinions surrounding the facts. As well as including some of my own, the opinions will be from sources such as the media and other fans. It is hoped that in taking this approach, it will serve as a vehicle through which to discuss the phenomena of — and the fan culture surrounding — Mk2.2 in a way that goes beyond being just a year-by-year account of what happened.

In such regard, as you're reading this book, you may find yourself disagreeing with some of the points made herein, but such is the nature of opinions. I only seek to put mine out there as food for thought. The intention isn't to explicitly change anyone's mind, or to insist that one opinion is superior to any other.

As a Deep Purple fan who was born in 1988, all of my knowledge and thoughts on the band are informed by, what is for me, an overview of the whole history. I didn't live through the excitement of the announcement that Mk2 would be making a comeback. I hadn't witnessed any of their 1970s live performances, or been around to witness the reactions when the albums from that period were released. Consequently, I feel that I am able to look at the whole of the Mk2.2 era through a historic lens — and *only* a historic one.

Does that make my opinion more neutral in how it can't have been tainted by any kind of nostalgic bias? Well, maybe. I'm not sure, to be honest. That's subjective, but for the purpose of transparency, it matters to me to state my position.

Within this book, I look forward to offering an exploration into the following questions: Was Deep Purple Mk2.2 really a good idea? Could they really cut it — commercially and creatively — in a music industry that looked so different to what it had been like in the 1970s? By the early eighties, with their respective careers in mind up to that point, did some band members need Deep Purple more than others? Was it good for fans to get the chance to see a phoenix rising from the ashes, or should the legend of the original Mk2 have been left to only the realms of speculation and fantasy?

Listen, Learn, Read On

By the early eighties, when talks of a reunion were no more than a fantasy in the minds of many fans, the name Deep Purple meant many different things to different people.

The band had, after all, gone through so many changes that to bear, for example, Deep Purple Mk4 in mind, was to invite a different train of thought compared to say, thinking about Mk2.

Come Taste The Band was wildly different to *Who Do We Think We Are*. Mk1's *Shades Of Deep Purple* was worlds away from Mk3's *Burn*. And so, by the early to mid-eighties, if you were to say to someone that Deep Purple would definitely reform, probably one of the first questions that would have come to mind was that of, "which one?".

By process of elimination, Mk4 was inevitably out of the equation due to the tragic passing of Tommy Bolin in December 1976, just over a year after the release of *Come Taste The Band* in October 1975. But let's have a Deep Purple equivalent of fantasy football for a moment; let's say that for the purpose of this discussion, Bolin hadn't tragically passed on and thus put a Mk4 reunion out of the equation.

What would an eighties version of this line-up have sounded like? For of course, no matter which line-up of Deep Purple would be the one to reunite, it was certain that they would need to be able to — to an extent — translate their sound into something that would be palatable, and indeed commercially viable, for a record-buying public that were listening to the likes of Wham!, The Human League, and

Michael Jackson (hold that last name in mind for a moment — I'm going to come back to that).

The artists I've listed there are perhaps an extreme example. The target audience for an eighties version of Deep Purple would have been more likely listening to music from other rock artists featured in *Kerrang!* — even where a lot of it was, for want of better term perhaps, mostly hair metal.

But let's look at who, musically, Deep Purple Mk4 were in 1975 when *Come Taste The Band* came out. The album was abundant in funk and soul influences, as was largely supported through Glenn Hughes', Tommy Bolin's, and — to an extent — David Coverdale's genre preferences at the time (Blackmore was out of the picture, having famously referred to the material on 1974's *Stormbringer* as "shoeshine music").

From *Come Taste The Band*, 'Gettin' Tighter', has an upbeat tempo. The funk and soul influence is largely there in the syncopated rhythms and Hughes' overall vocal approach. It's plausible to imagine that Michael Jackson could have easily sung on a similar-sounding track.

Imagine, for a moment, that the original Deep Purple vocals are removed from 'Gettin' Tighter', leaving just an instrumental backing track. Now, imagine that track perhaps a little higher in pitch to match Jackson's higher vocal range and in actual fact, the result isn't worlds away from what could have been — albeit in the realms of absolute fantasy and theory — a classic Michael Jackson track (if you're still in doubt, just listen to 'Gettin' Tighter' and imagine some trademark Jackson vocalisations being thrown in for good measure).

In saying the above, I hope I haven't ruined a classic Deep Purple song for anyone. What I'm getting at is this: had it been plausible that Mk4 Deep Purple was a viable option for the band's mid-eighties reunion, I would argue that it wouldn't have been beyond the realms of possibility for the band to have gone further into the whole funk and soul thing. By that point, a similar style of music had done commercial wonders for Michael Jackson. Would an eighties version of Deep Purple Mk4 have done well by trying to jump onto a similar bandwagon? Well, *maybe*, but it wouldn't have been without its problems.

In the seventies, many Deep Purple fans were disappointed that the Mk4 line-up of the band was, musically, so far removed from the likes of Mk2's *In Rock* and *Machine Head*, and even, Mk3's *Burn*. For those who saw Deep Purple as a name best associated with hard and heavy rock, for many, *Come Taste The Band* was not a good album. Even members of the band themselves said that the latter should not have been labelled as a Deep Purple album. It had, after all, made a significant departure from what many fans had perhaps been hoping for upon its release.

Now, I have yet to mention Jon Lord and Ian Paice with regards to *Come Taste The Band*. Even if a Mk4 reunion would have been possible in the mid-eighties, I would hazard a guess that those two would have been reluctant to participate.

As the two artists who had remained with every line-up of Deep Purple up to that point, I can't imagine that with all of the line-ups in mind, they would have been most pleased to make more albums and do more tours with that one. Taking Tommy Bolin's and Glenn Hughes' well-documented use of drugs out of the equation, and just considering the music, Lord had enjoyed a good working rapport with Ritchie Blackmore. Listen to their call and response moments and improvisations on some of the bootlegs of live performances from 1970.

As for Ian Paice, on *Come Taste The Band*, and indeed on Mk3's *Stormbringer*, it's clear that he could do all the funk-inspired rhythms with just as much talent, style and expertise as when he had played a heavier style on *In Rock* and *Machine Head*.

Looking back at his whole drumming career though, it's hard to imagine him not doing the whole heavy rock thing. His drumming alone on the title track of *Burn* pretty much says it all — a stellar performance and then some! (That said, the 1977 album — *Malice In Wonderland* — that Paice and Lord did with Tony Ashton is pretty abundant in funk and jazz styles.)

And what about David Coverdale? Well, I'll get to that in a bit when I discuss Mk3.

So, rewind for a moment. What about Mk1? Musically, I can't really imagine how that line-up of Deep Purple would have translated into the eighties. Considering the three albums that they put out in the late sixties — *Shades Of Deep Purple*, *The Book Of Taliesyn* and *Deep Purple* — I just can't comprehend how their original sound could have been developed into something commercially viable.

In fact, the music of Deep Purple Mk1 would have probably seemed like something of an ancient relic to the record-buying public of the eighties. I mean, how many bands were doing well with blues and long prog-rock-style solos by that point? If a band like Yes had to move into doing a song like 'Owner Of A Lonely Heart' to have a hit in 1983, then goodness only knows what leaps and bounds Deep Purple Mk1 would have needed to take in order to be a contender in the eighties. I say this as someone who very much enjoys the musical output of Deep Purple Mk1, but my point is that it was very much of its time. It has late sixties experimentation written all over it, really.

That scene from *Spinal Tap* springs to mind here: the one where they are performing '(Listen To The) Flower People' on a stereotypically-looking sixties TV show. It is awkward and uncomfortable, but they're just trying to fit in with the style of the day, and have yet to find that it's heavy rock that they really want to be doing.

Also on the Mk1 front, there's the personnel situation to be considered. Although every member of Mk1 was alive and well when the mid-eighties Deep Purple reunion happened, the odds of them being able to work happily and well together would have been tiny.

Singer Rod Evans was very much in the Deep Purple doghouse by that point. On Saturday 17th May 1980, he performed a gig at the Amarillo Civic Centre Auditorium in Texas to a crowd of around 1,400, which would have been fine in and of itself, but he chose to do so under the name of Deep Purple!

He had no legal right to do so, and when it was taken to court, this was acknowledged. Before the whole thing went to court, Evans had already been warned by HEC (Hire-Edwards-Coletta Enterprises — the rightful owners of the Deep Purple name) to cease performing under their trademark. It even saw one of HEC's other companies — Deep Purple (Overseas) Ltd. — taking out an advert in the *L.A. Times* the day before his gig at the Los Angeles' Long Beach Arena. Placed alongside the advert for Evans' gig, it stated that Blackmore, Glover, Lord, Paice, Hughes and Coverdale would not be performing at the show.

And what about bassist Nick Simper? Well, he has said even in relatively recent interviews that he is still pissed off about the way in which the Mk1 to Mk2 line-up change occurred in 1969. It's understandable too. Not only was he sacked, but the way in which it was done was brutal and very much behind his back. Everyone in the band — and even the management — knew that he was on his way out before he found out the hard way. Blackmore, Lord and Paice had already begun working with Gillan and Glover, all without his knowledge.

Hang on a moment though! It would be incredibly inaccurate to say that everyone in Deep Purple Mk2 was the best of friends in time for the mid-eighties reunion to happen.

More on that in a bit though, because for now, it is vital to add here that on the bassist front, Roger Glover was already working with Ritchie Blackmore. He had been playing in Blackmore's Rainbow for around five years by that point (having featured — and produced — on *Down To Earth, Difficult To Cure, Straight Between The Eyes* and *Bent Out Of Shape*).

If we are to argue, as many would have done at the time and throughout the entire decade of the seventies, that Blackmore is *the* Deep Purple guitarist, it surely makes sense that if he was to be a key component for a reunion line-up, that on bass, Glover should stick with him.

Sure, the two of them weren't joined at the hip. They had done plenty of work independently of each other. In 1973, Blackmore had even been instrumental in Glover's sacking from Deep Purple Mk2.1. Ever the professional though, it comes across that Glover is a man who can forgive and move on.

It has often been said that Glover has been the glue of Deep Purple Mk2; the man in the middle and the go-between for some of the more hot-headed personalities during a dispute (not to mention that musically, he has always been an ideas man, something which proved to be vital when he first joined Deep Purple for Mk2.1).

With Blackmore and Glover being forty percent of Mk2, it made absolute sense for that nucleus to be in the picture when it came to the decision that to front the Deep Purple reunion, Ian Gillan needed to be on vocals.

Right, yes, the vocalist decision, which of course, is a vital discussion point here, as in, "Why Mk2? Why not Mk3?"

I would argue that a Deep Purple reunion with David Coverdale back on lead vocals would have been an exciting choice for the mid-eighties. I mean, this is the Deep Purple that fans know and love from the iconic performance at the California Jam in 1974. This is the Deep Purple who brought us *Burn*. And sure, whilst the album that followed that, *Stormbringer*, was a very polarising one amongst fans, with tracks like 'Gypsy' and 'Soldier Of Fortune', could the musical stylings of this line-up have fared well in a mid-eighties reunion? Absolutely!

By 1984 when the Deep Purple reunion was in the works, commercially, David Coverdale would have seemingly been in a good position to abandon Whitesnake. Well, maybe "good position" isn't the nicest way of putting it.

He still wanted Whitesnake to do well, but around that time, following the release of their album *Slide It In*, the band was in turmoil and very much in a make-or-break situation. Sure, as hindsight now tells us, Coverdale found his magic formula for Whitesnake by targeting the music and performances towards an American audience. And wow, did it work for him!

Whitesnake's 1987 album was a huge success. But removing the advantage of hindsight from the equation for a moment, what we have is a plausible theory that maybe, just maybe, the Deep Purple mid-eighties reunion could have been one to feature Coverdale on vocals. After all, Jon Lord had been a member of Whitesnake since 1978, and had only just decided that staying with the band wasn't going to be for him. Could he, with Coverdale, have teamed up to make a move towards something more Purple-oriented?

Well, of his time in Deep Purple, Coverdale would go on to say in 1988; "It stopped being fun. There were five egomaniacs fighting for the spotlight, each feeling individually responsible for the success of the band, and it just stopped being a group. I checked out in March '76... The other day I spoke to Jon Lord, whom I have a great fondness for, and I was delighted to hear him sounding good about the way things were going.

He worked with me in Whitesnake, then left to re-join Purple, and he is the only member of Whitesnake to leave with my blessing. But for me, in those days, Deep Purple turned into a hard and uncomfortable job. Imagine working with people you don't like and with whom you don't share a common idea about where the music should be going — and the whole ego thing... I never really felt a part of the whole circus of Deep Purple."

Besides, Coverdale and Blackmore weren't on the best of terms — far from it, in fact! In February 1980, Blackmore and Coverdale had got into one hell of a fight. Having made some disparaging remarks about the guitarist to the press, the Whitesnake singer — who had apparently been invited by Cozy Powell — showed up backstage after a Rainbow gig. He did so in full knowledge that Blackmore wasn't happy with him. The result was two angry young(ish) men rolling around in a scuffle of long hair.

Hang on though! Was Blackmore even on the best of terms with Ian Gillan by the point at which the Deep Purple reunion was seriously being considered? It has been well documented that as members of Mk2.1, the two of them had an incredible rapport during the *In Rock* period, but pretty much thereafter, things started to take an uncomfortable turn to the point that, following a tense and unhappy period of working on *Who Do We Think We Are*, the singer handed in his notice.

However, when Blackmore was well into his tenure with his own band, Rainbow, he did actually jam on stage twice with Gillan: in 1978 at the Marquee, and again in March 1980 at London's Rainbow Theatre. On both occasions, Blackmore joined Ian Gillan and his band on stage for enthusiastic encores.

Overall, if we are to say that Blackmore was a definite candidate for Deep Purple's mid-eighties reunion, then it must be assumed that the guitarist would have been wanting to work with a vocalist with whom he had a good rapport. By that point, the revolving-door approach to line-ups that he had taken with Rainbow was such that clearly, he wouldn't have worked with just anyone. It would probably be fair to say though that Blackmore wasn't the best of friends with either Gillan or Coverdale. Both separate dynamics had had their sore points — both musically and personally.

By the early to mid-eighties, Gillan was well-placed to be very much up for a Deep Purple reunion.

Following his departure from Deep Purple Mk2.1 in 1973, he didn't perform until the Roger Glover-instigated Butterfly Ball in October 1975. "When I left Purple, it was like breaking up with a girl I was not only physically, but spiritually involved with," said Gillan. "And I felt so strongly about that at the time that I vowed — and in fact, it was in the newspapers — that I would never sing again. It's a statement I made at the time."

Gillan founded the Ian Gillan Band in 1975 alongside Ray Fenwick on guitar, Mike Moran on keyboards (later replaced by Mickey Lee Soule and then Colin Towns), Mark Nauseef on drums, and John Gustafson on bass. Their debut album, *Child In Time*, was released in July 1976, followed by *Clear Air Turbulence* in April 1977, and *Scarabus* in October of the same year. The band's sound was characterised by a jazz rock style that intrigued Gillan, but did not resonate with audiences, especially since punk rock was in vogue during that period.

Subsequently, Gillan formed another band under the name Gillan. It featured Colin Towns — who was responsible for co-writing most of the band's material — on keyboards. Additionally, the line-up included guitarist Steve Byrd, bassist John McCoy, and drummer Pete Barnacle.

However, Byrd and Barnacle were replaced by Bernie Tormé and Mick Underwood, a former member of Episode Six, after Gillan witnessed Tormé's performance with his punk trio.

Compared to Ian Gillan's previous band, this new group showcased a more robust hard rock sound, and their album *Mr. Universe*, released in October 1979, marked Gillan's return to the UK charts. However, the independent record label that released the album, Acrobat Records, went bankrupt shortly after, leading to a new agreement with Richard Branson's Virgin Records.

In 1980, Gillan released *Glory Road*. It resulted in the band making the first of several appearances on *Top Of The Pops*. Following the band's next album — *Future Shock* — Tormé left. His replacement, Janick Gers, appeared on the band's next two albums, *Double Trouble* and *Magic*.

Explaining that he needed to give his vocal cords a rest, much to the disappointment of the other musicians, Gillan decided that it was time to give up on the band.

In April 1983, Gillan officially became a member of Black Sabbath alongside founding members Tony Iommi, Geezer Butler and Bill Ward. As vocalist, Gillan was brought in to replace Ronnie James Dio.

"I had no plans to join Black Sabbath," Gillan explained. "We had talked about the reunion of Purple, but I knew that was at least two years away. I went out with Geezer and Tony, and we got drunk, and I found out the next day that I'd agreed to join the band."

The Gillan-fronted Sabbath set to work recording the *Born Again* album at the Manor Studios in Oxfordshire. Even by that point, he wasn't fitting in well with the band from a creative point of view on what would emerge to be the line-up's only album.

Drummer Bill Ward went on to say that he "didn't particularly like some of the lyrics that Ian was bringing forward and putting into the songs. Not because Ian doesn't write good lyrics or anything like that; I think Ian is an excellent performer, great singer and often at times I think his lyrics can be quite brilliant. But I just have a personal difference in what I like to hear in the way of lyrics, and so I felt terribly disconnected."

Gillan was unhappy with *Born Again*, so much so that rumour has it, upon being given a copy, he snapped the record and put it in the bin. "It's the worst produced album I've ever heard in my life!" he said. "If anyone could ever hear the demos of songs like 'Trashed' or 'Disturbing The Priest', it would throw a different light on it altogether. But Geezer Butler, unfortunately, dominated the post-production and the mixes were so bass-heavy it was virtually unplayable."

Due to health issues, Bill Ward opted not to join the rest of the band on the tour in support of *Born Again*. It resulted in former Move / ELO member Bev Bevan being brought in as a replacement.

As part of his role in Sabbath, Gillan needed to familiarise himself with the band's older songs. However, he struggled to remember the lyrics. His solution was to write them down on a Perspex folder, which he placed on the floor of the stage, flipping the pages using his feet.

It didn't really work though; the dry ice utilised on stage made it impossible for him to read the words, and the audience witnessed glimpses of him peering over the microphone to sing a few lines before vanishing below the dry ice to peruse the next set of lyrics.

As well as songs from *Born Again* and older Sabbath numbers, the band regularly played Deep Purple's 'Smoke On The Water', albeit for the encore.

Deciding that he didn't want to stay with Black Sabbath as a long-term prospect, Gillan quit after a second North American tour.

His time in the band wasn't necessarily bad from a social point of view. "We did an album and world tour and I loved every minute of it," he reflected. "It was the longest party I'd ever been to." Still though, musically, it seems that he still hadn't found a good fit for his talents following the end of his time with Deep Purple the first time around.

Now, Blackmore: in terms of whether or not committing to a Deep Purple reunion was an appealing option for him, that's a considerably different discussion. Compared to Gillan, Paice, Lord and Glover, the guitarist's career away from Deep Purple was arguably in that of a stronger position.

As a member of Blackmore's Rainbow, Glover didn't have the same extent of authority to make a decision on the band's future. The whole Rainbow situation leading up to the Deep Purple reunion certainly warrants further discussion.

Over The Rainbow

Not to disrespect any of the other members of Deep Purple Mk2, for of course, they have all had admirable and fruitful musical careers both with and away from the band. However, when it came to the particular period of time prior to the 1984 reunion, it could be argued that Ritchie Blackmore had the most to lose: a Deep Purple reunion would mean having to put Rainbow on the backburner.

As mentioned in the previous chapter, Paice, Gillan and Lord were all in something of a limbo with their own careers away from Deep Purple. Lord and Paice were both relatively fresh out of their stints in Coverdale's Whitesnake, whilst Gillan quit Black Sabbath in preparation for a Deep Purple reunion.

Glover had been with Rainbow since having been brought in to work on the *Down To Earth* album. Rightly or wrongly, his scope to stay with that band would have been subject to the decision of Blackmore.

It's amazing to think that in 1983, in terms of the scope for musical growth and creativity, Blackmore would have even considered calling it a day with Rainbow.

By this point in the band's tenure, although they were being discounted by many fans who preferred the Ronnie James Dio era, the fact is that commercially, Rainbow were on the up. Not only that, but with the 1982 album, *Straight Between The Eyes*, each musician had keenly advocated that everything was going well. Morale was good, and so was the creative rapport, enabling them to make music that they were pleased with.

When it came to making Rainbow's 1983 album, *Bent Out Of Shape*, another line-up change occurred in the form of Chuck Burgi replacing Bobby Rondinelli on drums. Apart from that though, the same team who had worked successfully together on *Straight Between The Eyes* remained: Blackmore, Turner, Glover, and keyboard player David Rosenthal.

Vitally, *Bent Out Of Shape* was a successful album. It got to a respectable number eleven in the UK chart, and to number thirty-four in the US. It spawned the singles 'Can't Let You Go' and 'Street Of Dreams'.

Videos were made for both, but it wasn't plain sailing. Dr Thomas Radecki of the National Coalition on Television Violence criticised MTV for airing the latter's accompanying video. Blackmore later went on to say that MTV banned it due to its hypnotism references.

Despite the fact that not all rock music fans were impressed with Rainbow by that point and considered them to have gone too far into sounding like a pop band, *Bent Out Of Shape* fared well when it came to the reviews.

From *Kerrang!*: "Hark! Listen to the dulcet tones of the Rainbow. Dig deep into the pockets, dispense with the necessary readies and prepare to be blown away! Yeah, this new Rainbow release follows *Straight Between The Eyes* as one excellent piece of plastic — it's thumbs up from me... But beware those of you who've just put the needle to *Rising* for the 8,000th time, while *Bent Out Of Shape* should indeed blow you away, it sure as hell ain't gonna cave your face in at the same time!"

"Y'see, as Ritchie Blackmore has been hinting for a good three years now, he certainly couldn't give a toss about being recognised as the world's greatest axe exponent anymore — at least not on vinyl. Nah, sensible chap that he is, Ritchie wants to be part of a group that's producing class rock 'n' roll

— no more, no less. For a guy with such a supposedly huge ego, he ain't letting it show through his Strat! Blackmore's breaks are short, concise, to the point, and, as such, far more effective than five-minute ramblings. Even the album's two instrumentals, 'Anybody There' and 'Snowman' are tunes in their own right, just as they should be!"

"Songs should be the key to anyone's heart and some sizeable locks could be opened here. With memorable moments in force, a weekend's spinning has been totally rewarding, revealing possibly Rainbow's most complete work to date. There's very little emphasis on performing to the standards required of a hard rock/heavy metal band, more in coming up with marvellous music and believe it or not, Rainbow mark eighty-seven (is it?) are infinitely superior when they keep it calm, keep it stealthy and don't worry too much about "rockin' out"."

"You'll get the drift when you compare newer-sounding Rainbow to older guard material. The former has produced two of this year's finest tunes, a double-headed delight on side B of this disc. 'Desperate Heart' stands out as the biggie, Joe Lynn Turner proving he's got as much in him as Lou Gramm (a compliment indeed!), while David Rosenthal shows that he has the necessary keyboard subtleties that are needed in this more mature Rainbow."

"Instant yet lasting, totally contemporary and a sophisticated joy to the ears — as is 'Street Of Dreams', the latest single criminally insulted by Chris Welch, taking up where 'Stone Cold' left off and carrying the style pretty much to ultimate perfection. Then there's 'Stranded', a spacey, keyboard-dominated opener that caresses you into submission. 'Can't Let You Go', where Joe Lynn Turner reveals his increasingly mature and sensitive lyrical capabilities, and 'Fool For The Night', a Blackmore/Turner composition which is as close to definitive modern day Rainbow as anything.

Minor quibbles concern 'Fire Dance' and 'Make Your Move', more on the old Rainbow pulse but too uninspired for such a generally well-crafted album, and also the fact that drummer Chuck Burgi hasn't been given the chance to really shine here. (Refer to Balance's *In For The Count* for a true reflection of his capabilities and quality). Minor quibbles indeed in terms of overall quality control. Now if Rainbow can carry that inspired atmosphere to the stage, we'll all be laughing — even Mr Blackmore might have to let a smile out. *Bent Out Of Shape*? Nah, Rainbow have trained hard — and they're in better shape than ever!"

Sounds considered; "*Bent Out Of Shape* is a beast of many moods, a mouth-watering multi-layered muesli of tempos and textures. Richer and more satisfying than *Straight Between The Eyes*, it recalls elements of *Rainbow Rising* as well as the later jukebox-rock that took Ritchie back to *Top Of The Pops*. Rock fans who can appreciate class as well as raw power will be well-served by this platter. Sure, there's plenty of melodic sensibility in evidence — but the crucial point is mass appeal doesn't necessarily equate with blandness. Some people make it into an art form and Blackmore could well be one of them. Crafty old Ritchie has found his top form again here, demonstrating with breathtaking ease why he, like so few others, genuinely deserves the epithet "Guitar Hero". Even at its gentlest, the album still sparkles thanks to his superb guitar-playing."

Melody Maker's review however was less encouraging: "Unfortunately, this LP is a virtual testament to the downfall of Ritchie Blackmore and his never-ending Rainbow. Sad but true. A detailed history lesson of the last few albums would prove the point adequately, but is rather unnecessary as every self-respecting Rainbow fan (past or present) will realise that the band peaked with *Rainbow Rising* and have slid backwards since... Ritchie Blackmore is still searching for that pot of gold and every time he releases a new album, he moves one step closer to total sell-out. Come on Ritchie, let's get back to basics."

Nevertheless, if the main objective of *Bent Out Of Shape* was to appeal to an audience in the US, it could be argued that it was a case of mission accomplished. In October 1983, Glover told *Melody Maker*; "The way you sell more records is to break America, and the way you break America is to get played on American radio. People say the band's gone soft, or gone commercial, but that's bullshit. The band has survived."

"Rainbow takes a surprising, if familiar, new stylistic turn," said *Billboard*. "Blackmore and chief writing partner Joe Lynn Turner, the band's vocalist, contribute songs in a more melodic pop/rock vein closer to Foreigner and Journey than Rainbow's usual peer group, while bassist Glover gives the production a crisp, sleek finish likewise aimed at AOR traditionalists. Songs like 'Stranded' and 'Can't Let You Go' could reap new airplay dividends as a result."

It could be said that overall, by 1983, Rainbow was everything that Blackmore had been hoping for when he had first decided to leave Deep Purple in 1975. He had achieved commercial success, whilst maintaining creative control. No longer was he at the whim of what other band members might have wanted to fight for in the studio (or indeed, anywhere else). For of course, when all was said and done, Rainbow was *his* band.

Ah, but that's where the problem with it came into the picture: arguably, one of money.

From the very beginnings of Rainbow, Blackmore was largely responsible for funding the band himself, which he was able to do with his earnings from Deep Purple. He had enthusiastically chosen creative freedom over and above the guaranteed paycheque of being in an established — and incredibly successful — band.

Whilst the younger Blackmore was in a position to take that risk, the Blackmore of 1983 was financially in a very different situation: he was going through an expensive divorce.

As for the rest of the 1983 Rainbow line-up, the truth of the matter was that really, a secure future with the band just didn't come as one of the perks of the job.

Even after the release of *Straight Between The Eyes*, perhaps really, there was little that could be done to ensure the continuation of Rainbow thereafter. As tour manager Colin Hart recalled, *Bent Out Of Shape* was the album that Blackmore made with a particular goal in mind; "Bruce [Payne — Rainbow's manager] had always kept in touch with Phil Banfield, Ian Gillan's personal manager, and more than once I heard the rumour around the office that the two of them were "in a huddle" over, if not a complete reunion of Deep Purple, at least a one-off concert with the fabled line-up... The rumours of a Purple reunion persisted until March when Ritchie told me he would have one last attempt at breaking Rainbow. I was mystified as we were a massive draw in most markets, were we not already "broken"? Just what was he after? The albums, although not triple-platinum, still sold in considerable number and the tours were always pretty much sold out in most venues. He had the respect of virtually every musician you could shake a stick at, and Bruce had ensured his personal wealth was not only intact, but also expanding. In truth, he was not exactly unhappy, more restless and ill at ease. I guess the word was "unfulfilled"." (It is worth noting that *Straight Between The Eyes* eventually went silver in the UK).

It's clear that Blackmore wasn't drastically unhappy with Rainbow in and of itself. Testament to that is in how he would go on to bring Joe Lynn Turner back on vocals for Deep Purple's 1990 album, *Slaves And Masters*.

Of course, as many fans of Rainbow would plausibly

agree, would a follow-up to *Bent Out Of Shape* have been a welcome addition to the band's discography? Absolutely! Tracks like 'Can't Let You Go' and 'Make Your Move' are demonstrative of how the band were going strong around that time. 'Street Of Dreams' clearly shows that there was no absence of emotion in Blackmore's playing and indeed, the originality of writing with Joe Lynn Turner and Roger Glover.

With Blackmore deciding to commit to a Deep Purple reunion, it makes absolute sense that Glover came along too. The latter was a key contributor to Rainbow, and has been a close friend of Ian Gillan since their pre-Purple days with Episode Six.

Although many fans would have been sad to hear about the end of Rainbow, the announcement of a Deep Purple reunion would be a treat for many. Besides, Rainbow went out in style. On 14th March 1984 in Japan, they were accompanied by an orchestra for a spellbinding version of 'Difficult To Cure'. Fortunately, it was filmed for video release.

It was by the time that Blackmore was back in the Deep Purple fold that he would speak more candidly about the decision to call it a day with Rainbow: "Although Rainbow did some good stuff, it didn't ever have the identity that Purple has. Sometimes with Purple, I'll hear the end product and maybe think it should have been more like this or that, but it's always very popular with the masses. With Rainbow, I had everything more or less how I wanted to hear it, but it didn't appeal as much to the masses, so there's obviously something I'm not tapping into, the pulse of the masses. I don't feel that I was wrong — I had to do something on my own — but the popularity of Rainbow compared to Purple shows me that I'm not right all the time. With Rainbow, I had it all my way, totally one-hundred percent, but now Ian Gillan, who is definitely not a normal person, ha!, will come up with the melodies and lyrics to things I've written which I would never have thought of. That's part of the chemistry and magic of Purple."

When asked if he regretted calling it a day with Rainbow, the guitarist said; "Generally, I was pleased with the way things were going. I was going through a melodic phase... At the end, I was kind of faced with a great dilemma with Rainbow: should we carry on doing ballads or get back to rock? I enjoyed the band's softer phase; 'Stone Cold', 'Street Of Dreams' and stuff like that, I really liked, but it died a death, particularly in Britain, which hurt a lot, because it means a lot to me to be successful in my home country. So in the end, I got very frustrated, and that's when the first really serious thoughts of a Purple reformation entered my head."

"[Ritchie] left for Rainbow because he wanted to be in charge, which he wasn't in Deep Purple, and so he put his print on Rainbow's music," Glover went on to say in 1985. "Back in Deep Purple, he is and was the main instigator of the music, so there's definitely a point of comparison. But there's a whole different attitude in the way Deep Purple plays together. Jon and Ritchie feed off each other, and me and Paice do too. It's like a corporate identity, in a way, not just like a bunch of musicians playing a song together. Deep Purple has an identity as a band. Maybe that's what Rainbow always lacked. Rainbow was a popular band, but it never had that elusive hit record. It reached its plateau, and for the last three or four years, it made all the right moves without getting further along. It just went on from year to year, and for me, at least, there was a sense of just marking time. Initially, I tried to get out of that by doing solo albums, and I certainly had no thoughts of a Deep Purple reunion. In fact, I was actually against it for a long time, feeling that Deep Purple was not a band so much as an era. But I've changed my mind."

Who Do We Think We Are

On 13th April 1984, whilst Jon Lord was still on tour with Whitesnake in Scandinavia, he got a phone call from Blackmore inviting him to a meeting. When the original Mk2 members met up shortly after in Greenwich, Connecticut, although they hadn't lost touch prior to that, it was the first time that all five of them had been in a room together since June 1973 in Japan.

"It was vaguely embarrassing at first," said Lord. "There was lots of 'Hi, how've you been?'. Then we noticed we were all smiling, and I think it was Ritchie who said, 'Well, are we going to do it or what?' And everyone said 'Yeah'. We talked for twenty minutes about the basis on which we would get back together, then we finally said, 'Enough talk. Let's just do it'. It seemed like the best idea at the time… It was a combination of things that really made us do it. The enthusiasm of Ian Gillan, combined with the realisation that none of us had been having as much fun in the intervening years as we thought we had, or that we did have, before."

"It had to be this line-up," said Blackmore. "Because in my book, I think the most creative we ever were, the most identity we ever established, was with this exact line-up. Obviously it could have been any line-up, because they would have all been there quick enough, no matter what they say! But it was established years ago that this had to be it. There is an identity that this Purple has that I didn't find with all the other members of Rainbow... After seven or eight years of doing that, I've got it out my system. And I think they've done the same thing. There's still a great — I won't say "spark" because it's a great flame — within the Purple line-up that we have; there is a chemistry within these five people, some sort of rhythm. It's a pulse, and it does work. That helps."

Jon Lord simply said of the Mk2 line-up, "This is the right one. This is Deep Purple".

A week after the initial meeting, the Mk2 folk met up again in New York, at manager Bruce Payne's Thames Talent offices. It was there that they officially agreed to reform Deep Purple, and that this would result in both recordings and a tour.

By 1984, Deep Purple's original management team of Tony Edwards and John Coletta were no longer in the frame to take control of the band a second time around. Ironically, it was Edwards and Coletta who had originally invested in Bruce Payne and set up Thames Talent so that they could have more control and a share in the earnings from the US agency employed to book Deep Purple's concerts from 1974 onwards.

Prior to that, Payne had been working for the ATI Agency that had been booking Purple's US concerts. Essentially, he became part of the Purple organisation once Thames Talent was incorporated.

Although Edwards and Coletta had parted company, they still had to oversee the running of the Purple back catalogue and all that entailed with royalties etc. Edwards was running his new creation — Safari Records — and Coletta had been managing Coverdale and Whitesnake. That, however, was just coming to an end as Coverdale wanted out of the contract.

On account of the latter, and with the personal relationship between Edwards and Coletta all but broken, it was never feasible that the pair would reunite to manage Deep Purple again.

However, it must have been galling for both of them not to be involved individually. In particular, Coletta had tried to put together a one-off reunion shortly after the split in 1976. However, at the time, Jon Lord had no intention of getting involved. As he explained in 1978; "It was begun to be planned a year or so ago. It was done by Martini Rosso. Martini, a merchant bank, and someone else wanted to finance a big concert in Ibiza and they asked our old management, who asked us individually. But I don't think there's any need for Deep Purple to come together again. You've got six or seven people to take care of, and every one of these people have their own career to be concerned about. I'm more concerned with Whitesnake being correct and successful and making good music than I am with putting something back together that is in the past anyway."

Clearly in the intervening years, Lord's viewpoint had changed.

Blackmore said, "When we first got back together, I remember wondering, 'Will it work in the eighties, will it be in vogue with what's going on?'. And then I thought, 'Sod it, who cares? Let's just go ahead and do it anyway'."

News of the reunion first hit the UK media on Friday 27th April. It was reported in London's *Evening Standard*, and then confirmed the same day by Tommy Vance on his BBC Radio One *Friday Rock Show*. He made a fun game of it by playing some of the band's songs and inviting the listening audience to guess which rock band he was talking about. Having spoken to Ian Gillan the day before, Vance was in a position to confirm the news.

The news of the reunion was met with all kinds of responses. The word "dinosaurs" cropped up quite a lot, and there were accusations that the band was doing it for a quick cash-in. "There had been a long gap from 1976 to 1983, and during those seven years there had been various blandishments," said Lord. "We were offered a-million-and-a-half bucks to do one album and a concert — I mean *each*! This was in 1981. So you can see the prime mover behind reforming was not financial. If that had been the reason, we would have done it before. We got back together for a far less starry figure."

In interviews, everyone in the band would go on to insist that the cynics had got it wrong, but really, the judgement would have to be on the music. For cynics and enthusiasts alike, it was clear that Deep Purple would need to come up with the goods. With such classics as *In Rock* and *Machine Head* to their name, could they do it again? After all, they had one hell of a reputation — and indeed, legend — to live up to.

On 1st May 1984, Deep Purple Mk2 began full rehearsals. Based in Northern Vermont, their gear was set up at The Base Lodge on an estate owned by the Von Trapp family. It resulted in Blackmore (perhaps with tongue firmly in cheek) suggesting that the new album should be called *The Sound Of Music*. The first few days in the studio were spent jamming, the purpose being to get the band used to playing together again.

"We went to Vermont, to a little hideaway," said Glover. "We set up the equipment in the basement of a big old house and spent a couple of weeks jamming together. And that's when the material started coming out. From that, we decided to make a record, which we recorded in the same place we rehearsed it. When we started playing music together, I realised that there was a chemistry that flows among the five of us that just couldn't be denied."

It was from this that more established ideas for new material came. A lot of the jams were recorded. It enabled them to be played back for reference and development into songs. In particular, Blackmore brought lots of new ideas to the table — and notably, the riffs.

"Ritchie was brimming with ideas, which were used,"

said Glover. "Ian Gillan and I do the lyrics. Everybody contributes stuff. It just flowed." ('Wasted Sunsets' — or at least, an embryonic form of it — was very much Blackmore's and Glover's. When they were in Rainbow, in late 1980, they recorded takes of a song by this name at Sweet Silence Studios in Copenhagen.)

The band had set themselves the goal of getting enough material together for an album within the space of a month. "We had a great time discovering each other again," said Glover. "The music flowed very easily. The only intention was for us to be us, and not pretend to be somebody else. Whatever we did in the early days that made the music successful was done with complete disregard for anything else. Whatever kind of music we made, that was it. I was very concerned that this album should be a completely natural album. Because there's no leader in Deep Purple, the resulting music is a compromise among five people fighting and pushing for what they want, and we've all had an influence in it. I was very pleased with the way we wrote songs in much the same way as we used to."

It was during this time that, using a home video camera, Bruce Payne filmed the band working together. The footage would later be used in promotional videos. All whilst this was happening, everyone involved avoided the press. As they did so, news of the reunion was promoted in the general media and by the music press around the world, for of course, the news of Deep Purple's reunion was vital.

After having got off to a flying start, June 1984 was a somewhat slower month for the band. With rehearsals having come to an end at the start of the month, the plan had been to go straight on to recording the album in a mobile studio at The Base Lodge. However, the authorities in Vermont turned down the band's application to do so. The result was some time off whilst another location was sorted out.

Still though, it wasn't a holiday by any means, for it was

during this time that the band began to open up to the press.

"We're all totally committed to this band, this is not a one-time arrangement," said Jon Lord. "We plan on recording and touring regularly."

"I am totally committed to this project, and I'm determined to make Purple as successful as we once were," said Blackmore, adding, "Rainbow is simply on hiatus. There may be additional efforts with the band, there may not. At this point I cannot say."

By the mid-eighties, were the members of Mk2 better placed to handle the challenges of being in such a high-profile band? It's hard to tell, but the intent to embrace the years of experience behind them certainly seemed to be there.

"Suddenly things moved very fast," Gillan said of Mk2's first round of success in the early seventies. "We didn't have any spare time left. Everything we touched turned to gold. There was an amazing amount of money coming in, which we had no time to spend in a sensible way. So we just lived it up, not thinking of the consequences. At a certain moment it went to our heads, and we split up. We were too young for such big success… All five of us have learned a great deal. You might say that we have grown up. After Purple broke up, we all had to take a few steps back — which was a good thing. We now know that success does not come naturally. You have to work very hard for it. Even then it is not guaranteed."

"We've realised how basically stupid some of the things we did in the old days were," said Lord. "Because we're ten years older than we were then, it makes a lot of difference. It's easier to look at each other and respect each other for what we are, and what we've become."

"Youth helps to create something new, but it can also destroy you," said Blackmore. "Inexperience is almost a synonym for self-destruction."

On 6th July, the band moved to Horizons, a large house in

Stowe close to where they had been rehearsing. Tour manager Colin Hart had organised it by networking with local real estate agents. Before Jon Lord was able to get his gear sorted and in place (much of which needed to be renewed anyway), for the initial rehearsals, the band had used mostly Rainbow's gear — including a Hammond organ, keyboards and cabinets all owned by Blackmore.

With everything set up and with the French Canadian-owned 'Le Mobile' mobile studio ready for use, the band began the recording sessions — which would continue for six weeks — on 10th July. 'Under The Gun' was recorded quickly, but 'The Unwritten Law' was put on the backburner and wouldn't be developed further until the next album.

Despite the fact that the media and the fans only had Deep Purple's previous work to go on, promoters were already eager to know where the band would first be playing in Britain. Until it was decided that the capacity was too small to host Deep Purple, the Reading Festival in August had widely been reported as the venue of choice. The rumour mill had also included mention of the Milton Keynes Bowl. Finally, the rumours were put to rest once Bruce Payne made an official statement that Deep Purple would not be performing at an outdoor venue any time soon.

Outside of the band, Roger Glover's solo album, *Mask*, was released. It had been recorded a year earlier, but due to the Deep Purple reunion that overshadowed it (or helped to draw attention to it, depending which way you look at it), he didn't have time on his side to do any significant amount of promotion. Still though, *Music Week* asserted that the album was "more in line with Peter Gabriel than heavy rock" and "deserves to do well".

The recording sessions for *Perfect Strangers* came to an end on 26th August. Jon Lord claimed that the band had recorded more material than was actually needed for an album, although this is perhaps debatable on the basis that if additional material does exist, it has never seen the light of day.

Something the band did speak about at the time though, was on the amount of jams they did. One of them, 'Son Of Alerik', initially saw release as a single B-side. The ten-minute jam occurred when a film crew was present. Whilst waiting for the crew to set the equipment up, Blackmore started an improvisation, and Glover, Lord and Paice soon joined in. Glover's recollection was that Blackmore kept it going for a while, just to annoy the film crew!

Two other jams that have also circulated amongst collectors are 'RIJIR' and 'Cosmic Jazz'. 'RIJIR' is a blues shuffle, whereas 'Cosmic Jazz' showcases a vastly different side to Purple. It was inspired by a discussion about how a lot of modern jazz appears to sound as though the musicians aren't listening to one another; it was this idea that prompted Purple to jam in that style on this extraordinary piece.

Still not giving any official interviews, and with no official record deal in place, the band got ready to fly out to Hamburg. On 1st September, they got together at Hamburg's Tennessee Tonstudio. Prior to mixing the album, they added overdubs to what had been recorded in the US.

Roger Glover served on production duties. He had been reluctant to do so originally, asserting that a neutral influence would be the best option. It was the case, however, that the rest of the band trusted him and felt that he was the man for the job.

In terms of writing credits, the only track on *Perfect Strangers* credited to the whole band was 'Nobody's Home', despite Gillan and Glover having stipulated that they would have preferred to use the same all-for-one approach to composition credits that Mk2 had originally used for their 1970s albums. For the Mk2 reunion, it was Blackmore's preference to attribute writing credit to individual band members, a practice that would continue within the band up until 1993 upon his departure.

The thorny issue of writing credits stemmed back to the beginnings of the band. When 'Hush' was a major hit in the States, Jon Lord and Rod Evans made more money from the single due to having composed the B-side, 'One More Rainy Day'.

When Gillan and Glover joined the band in 1969, Blackmore in particular was insistent that all the songs should be credited to all band members. This set-up still didn't guarantee a happy band though; the guitarist was less than pleased upon claiming that Lord wasn't even present for the writing of 'Strange Kind Of Woman'.

When Gillan and Glover were replaced by Coverdale and Hughes, although for contractual reasons Hughes couldn't put his name to any songs, Blackmore saw himself as the main composer and made sure this was reflected on the credits for *Burn*.

By 1984, the guitarist's preference on how band members should be credited was not necessarily down to him not being a team player — a vital consideration owing to what some might say when embracing a retrospective narrative towards all things Purple. "Everybody is as important as the next person," he said.

"There's always favourites from the fans. But there's five very strong musicians, and that's how I like to leave that. I write the foundation of a song, and construction and the riffs, and the general shape of the song. Roger will put in some of the refinements, some of the lyrics, and he's very important on the production side. He's very happy in that vein — that's far too tedious for me. I can't stand pushing phasers for sixteen hours a day. I had too much of studios way back. I did a lot of sessions and I'm sick of seeing the inside of a studio."

It was in September that the album's title of *Perfect Strangers* was announced, and that the band had signed a record deal with Polygram. The first official publicity photographs of the band were taken. They would ultimately make an appearance on the album's back cover. Unexpectedly, the group also played a short set one evening at a Hamburg nightclub (an image of which would also make an appearance on the inner sleeve of *Perfect Strangers*). "We were all in a great mood, and that was the first time we've actually played in ten years on stage," said Blackmore. "The name kind of got a few people thinking; but they were more interested in ordering the first beer."

By October, Mk2 were rehearsing in England for their tour. They did so at St Peter's Hall — at the time, a private members club — in Bedford (Stuart Smith, who was working as an assistant to Blackmore, had previously lived in the area). It was the location of choice in terms of how the band wished to keep a low profile for the purpose of what they wished to achieve. There for two weeks, as well as working on the new material, they used this time to re-learn the *Made In Japan*-era setlist.

Glover said: "Throughout the making of *Perfect Strangers* and throughout the jam sessions before it, we never once played any of the old tunes. Not one single bit. No 'Lazy', no nothing. We went to England to rehearse — a town called Bedford — specifically to learn the old stuff. And I remember we started 'Highway Star'. We figured we couldn't possibly have started our live show without it being 'Highway Star'. And the beginning is easy enough to remember, but by the time we got to the chord changes for the solos, the whole thing fell apart. None of us could remember, so it was like, 'Get the roadie. Is there a record shop around here somewhere?'. We had to go out and buy the record to relearn the songs!"

As part of Polygram's promotional operations, the band

was interviewed by Tommy Vance — not just for his own show, but for a promotional album to be syndicated for play on American radio stations.

Whilst in Bedford, the band played football with some of the locals. Thereafter, some members travelled up to Merseyside for a charity match organised by Liverpool's Radio City, whose DJ Phil Easton had also interviewed the band in Bedford. His interview with Lord and Gillan was used as a promotional album for Polygram in the UK. At the end of the month, Deep Purple went back to the US to participate in an international press launch in New York.

With the album now out on LP, cassette and CD, the first batch of tour dates were set. The plan was to get going in Australia and New Zealand, with the first date set for Perth on 27th November. Regarding the decision, Lord said, "We thought we'd better go a long way away, and if we get it wrong, it's far enough away from home, isn't it! By the time we get into Europe and specifically the UK, I want this to be so hot."

With the full stage set decided upon, the band undertook another two weeks of rehearsal in America. Gillan and Lord made a brief trip back to the UK for an appearance on *Whistle Test* (previously titled *The Old Grey Whistle Test*).

Press enthusiasm for the album was contagious, with large posters in every UK city and an abundance of media advertising in place overall. *Music Week* reported in October 1984; "Described at the Polygram sales conference as 'one of the first heavy metal bands', the reformed Deep Purple feature as a Polygram priority for the winter season. Promotion includes a fifteen-minute documentary on how the band came to reform, which is being filmed for television use; interviews from their New York press conference for broadcast on Radio One on October 26th; and extensive editorial press coverage. Polygram stresses that this is not a one-off — the band has signed a four-album deal and they will be touring Australia in November, the US next February, and the UK next spring."

Released in October 1984, across many countries in Europe, *Perfect Strangers* quickly hit the top five. It got to number four in Japan. The band had always had a loyal following there — as had Blackmore, which had proven to be the case when he'd toured there with Rainbow. It got to number five in the UK and to number seventeen in the US — pretty good going, not just for a reunion band, but considering that the record was in a genre of music that wasn't the most dominant in the charts on either side of the Atlantic by the mid-eighties. When it went platinum in the US, it was the first of Deep Purple's albums to do so since *Machine Head*.

Overall, the reviews were pretty decent too! Notably, the more cynical ones generally came from the more mainstream music press (rather than specialist rock publications and local newspapers featuring contributions from journalists with a broader passion for music).

The Los Angeles Times praised *Perfect Strangers* as "an LP that stands up well alongside [Deep Purple's] best collections".

From *The San Francisco Examiner*: "Despite the initial scepticism that greeted news of Deep Purple's rebirth, *Perfect Strangers* re-introduces a grown-up, more technically adept group, still intact, yet venturing into less shrapnel-filled territory. The points of reference though — Blackmore's howling, Lord's cathedral embellishments, and Gillan's soulful wails — will return the seasoned listener immediately to rock's raucous past."

From *Rolling Stone*: "The title track comes blasting out of nowhere, like an I'm-alive-and-well message from an old friend you'd given up for dead. With its steamy vocal and genuine, if uncharacteristic, touches of wit throbbing above Deep Purple's heavy signature sound, *Perfect Strangers* sets the tone for this venerable band's reunion album. Lead singer Ian Gillan — who's never been in finer, and deeper, throat — sinuously glides into lyrics that suggest these veterans have something to say about where they've been in the last few years ('Can you remember, remember my name... I am the echo of your past') and have lots more to offer in the future. For a moment, you almost wonder why Purple ever faded away in the first place. Until, that is, you hear the rest of the album."

"Excepting the title cut and the rambunctious but less effective 'Knocking At Your Back Door', the material consists of hastily knocked-off jams that allow guitar demigod Ritchie Blackmore to whip out his finger exercises in public. The band spent about six to eight weeks recording this comeback. (The current line-up is actually neither the original nor the final Deep Purple but the most successful — of 'Smoke On The Water' fame.) It doesn't sound as if they spent much more time thinking about it, either."

"Blackmore's Strat has such a great roar that you're willing to just let it reverberate in your eardrums for a bit. And it's nice to hear Jon Lord's unsynthesised organ squalls, Ian Paice's meaty pounding, Gillan's howls and whispers and Roger Glover's solid bass lines once again. Eventually, though, it's "enough of the sound check already — where are the songs?". Instead of Glover, an outside producer might have forced the band to tighten up its licks and arrangements. Then again, did Deep Purple ever have more than one or two really good, concise numbers on an album? Maybe they're just making the kind of record they always did, the only kind they know how to make."

"So why are they doing this? To cash in on the current heavy-metal craze, in which dozens of young upstarts are making fortunes playing Purple riffs? Following a recent meet-the-press shebang promoting the album and impending world tour, the band members (minus the temperamental Blackmore, who, true to his "enigmage", didn't show) insisted they don't need the dough. Perhaps the answer lies in 'Wasted Sunsets', a portrait of an aging rock star who's got 'gold and silver for the blues' but nothing to do except drink the nights away. It's nice that *Perfect Strangers* got the Purples out of their respective mansions; too bad they didn't venture farther from home."

With regards to the overall sound on *Perfect Strangers*, Blackmore said in 1985; "Deep Purple is a hostage to its image, it's a kind of stereotype. Ian should sing like this, I have to play like that, the same with Jon. Fans expected this from us, and for us it's completely natural to play like that. This is the magic of Deep Purple... Deep Purple records are bought in order to hear Deep Purple. We will not change. We are a band from the seventies and we play rock from the seventies. Despite the fact that it's the eighties, I don't want to imitate modern rock."

From *Billboard*: "Contrary to the jacket blurb, it's probably career timing, not destiny that sparked this bona fide reunion for Messrs. Glover, Blackmore, Gillan, Lord and Paice, who reconstitute the original late sixties hard rock blueprint with surprising punch. With Gillan's prototypical vocal leaps, Blackmore's fevered guitar and Lord's surging organ fills, this is AOR revivalism that should click, thanks to a major tour and the rekindled metal market."

From *Cash Box*: "The saga of Deep Purple took a welcome turn for fans of their unique style of rugged hard rock when the group reunited recently. *Perfect Strangers* is sure to recapture old and win over new admirers of this British band... Illness and internal friction led to the band's break-up in June of 1976, and its members pursued separate careers as soloists or with other groups. Now, however, Deep Purple is most assuredly back, and its new album is up-to-date and yet still in the best tradition of its previous work, making it seem to many as if the band never left at all."

CMJ New Music Report listed the album as a "Killer Pick", saying, "What did you expect? When it comes to producing excellence in hard rock, you don't mess with the guys who invented it. Although *Perfect Strangers* combines the bluesy Purple style with a touch of vintage Rainbow, it is not in the least dated. Guitarist Ritchie Blackmore is at his prime, adding his distinctive classically influenced leads over Jon Lord's haunting array of keyboards. The incredible title track is the killer choice with 'Knocking At Your Back Door' and 'Hungry Daze' close seconds. If there were more so-called dinosaur bands like this, the species wouldn't be extinct." (It's interesting how this review doesn't seem to use the term "dinosaur bands" as an insult, but simply in reference to the fact that the band has an established history behind them).

From *The St Louis Post Dispatch*: "The record bristles with white-hot intensity from beginning to end. The songs are among the best in the band's history, and the legendary musicianship of the group appears to be intact. One playing convinces the listener that not only is Deep Purple back, but the band is better than ever."

The band started their tour in late November 1984. Covering New Zealand and Australia first, the schedule was kept relatively flexible, allowing for extra dates to be added to accommodate demand. Some lucky fans even got to play football with the band on days off.

At this stage, the setlist consisted of a blend of classics and new songs: 'Highway Star', 'Nobody's Home', 'Strange Kind Of Woman', 'A Gypsy's Kiss', 'Perfect Strangers', 'Under The Gun', 'Knocking At Your Back Door', 'Lazy', 'Child In Time', Rainbow's 'Difficult To Cure', 'Space Truckin''. 'Smoke On The Water' and 'Black Night' were used for encores. The band was given a warm welcome overall.

Inevitably, the band were still getting warmed up after having been away for so long. Still though, with the setlist including a fair bit of new material, they clearly didn't want to rely on just the old favourites. That's not to say though, that there was an absence of nostalgia — or at least, the feeling that it was great to be back together. During the band's performance at Adelaide Memorial Drive on 30th November, Gillan introduced 'Speed King' as part of the encore, saying "we haven't done this song in eleven years".

The journalist who reviewed the performance at Adelaide's Memorial Drive was already a Blackmore fan, having obtained a fragment of the man in black's guitar during an end-of-show smashing in 1976. They wrote with candour, "I must admit that I was swept along with the other Purplites to the old Memorial on a late Friday afternoon and saw the spectacle: The Marshall stacks, the huge Paice kit, the famous organ with Jon Lord emblazoned on the side — only twenty yards away. I had this queasy, thrilling feeling. I mean, it's one thing digging these guys when you're a school kid. What happens ten years on, when you're, of course, older, discerning and wiser and totally pissed off with the final Purple line-up and the solo jaunts of the last decade... Crash! There they were, suddenly blasting into 'Highway Star', just the way they'd done it on *Made In Japan*. The crowd was on its feet, braying its approval."

"By midway through the first song, Purple had already proven themselves to be more than old men clutching at faded memories. This was a Purple that was fresh and raring to go, Ian Gillan and Blackmore actually laughing and exchanging vocal guitar routines... The solos were out tonight, oh yes — Blackmore on a stunning 'Space Truckin'', Ian Paice on 'Lazy', and Jon Lord on 'Song Of Joy' (sic), a tribute to Blackmore's strong love for classical music. The first highlight of the evening came with 'Speed King', the archetypal Purple song with Gillan in fine screaming tone and Blackmore spraying the front rows with magic, followed by 'Black Night', as tight and dynamic as you'd have wanted them to be. Once they reached a high, they kept that throughout the encore through 'Space Truckin'' and the teasing 'Smoke On The Water'. Purple proved that comebacks can work, and Ritchie Blackmore proved that in a band of good players he was outstanding — both as instrumentalist and showman. The only disappointing aspect of the performance, actually, was that he didn't smash up his trusty axe."

The journalist also noted how whilst the support band — a local group called Ironhorse — was good enough, the crowd was only excited by one Ritchie Blackmore taking a peek out from backstage during their set. Although it took Purple a while to start playing due to a few technical issues, the journalist insisted that it was very much worth it.

A review of one of the performances at Brisbane's Festival Hall said that "the music of Deep Purple is as strong as ever", that they "won the crowd", and that the title track of the new album was "well received".

George Harrison made a special guest appearance at the Sydney gig on 13th December. A close friend of Jon Lord, he joined the band on stage to play 'Lucille' after having been out of the public eye for quite a while by that point.

One journalist wrote of the band's performance in Sydney; "Their musicianship was extraordinary and their sound has not dated a bit since this line-up split". They considered that when the reunion was announced in April, it seemed that it "would be just another revivalist novelty in the money-spinning mould of Chuck Berry and The Troggs" but that this was "not so: Deep Purple have returned to play their oldies with joy and panache, and are keen to find acceptance for material off their new album. The band has a new generation to play to — one that flaunts black AC/DC, Saxon, and Iron Maiden t-shirts —

BEATLE ROCKS SYDNEY AGAIN

By BRETT THOMAS

EX-BEATLE George Harrison stunned rock fans at the Sydney Entertainment Centre last night when he jumped on stage to play with the rock group Deep Purple.

It was the first time Harrison has played on an Australian stage since the fabulous Beatles tour of 1964.

Harrison, dressed in a white suit, ambled on from the side of the stage as singer Ian Gillan introduced the re-formed Deep Purple to the crowd during the first encore.

Gillan gave the microphone to Harrison — and the lead guitarist from rock's greatest band introduced himself to the capacity crowd as "Arnold from Liverpool ... NSW."

Gillan kept the joke going, telling the audience "Arnold" had won a contest to play with the band.

What followed was a sizzling few minutes as the band and Harrison jammed on the old Little Richard classic Lucille — with the ex-Beatle taking over lead guitar from Deep Purple's Ritchie Blackmore.

Those in the audience who recognised the now reclusive guitarist cheered and screamed as they watched history being made.

When the song was over, Harrison walked off stage as quietly as he had come on, while Deep Purple asked the crowd to "thank George for playing with us."

Harrison, a close friend of Deep Purple's Ian Paice and Jon Lord, is in Australia to launch his book Fifty Years Adrift which is about the history of the Beatles and the music of the 60s and early 70s.

Deep Purple, who were among the first of the "heavy metal kings", have started their world-wide reformation tour in Australia, 11 years after they split up. They play their last Sydney show tonight at the Entertainment Centre.

Deep Purple vocalist Ian Gillan

PULSE

Harrison steps out with Purple ...

Deep Purple fans at the Sydney Hordern Pavilion were given a bonus — when the legendary George Harrison stepped out of the wings to join the band on "Lucille".

It was the first time that Harrison — introduced onstage as "Alf" — had been on a stage for ten years.

Harrison was in Australia to help launch a book by his former publicist Derek Taylor at a $60-a-head luncheon at the Sydney Opera House.

Wearing a two-piece grey suit and an Hawaiian shirt, Harrison chatted to more than 200 people, including members of INXS, Mondo Rock and QED, leading business persons and advertisers and Beatles fanatics who'd come from all over Australia — including one guy with a car bonnet with Beatles' pictures on it which he wanted George to sign (imagine the strange looks he got when carrying it on the bus trip from Adelaide to Sydney).

Over the last few years Harrison has locked himself away in his mansion on Oxfordshire. He won't tour any more, after Lennon's murder, and although he writes songs, he says he doesn't feel the need to commit them to an album. "The whole Beatles' thing just seems like a vague memory — like it was in a precious incarnation," he said, before adding that after his autobiography *I Me Mine* and Taylor's *Fifty Years Adrift*, he would no longer involve himself in any more Beatles' projects. Of all the ex-members, Harrison has been most contemptuous of the Beatles' myth.

After hustling himself for twenty years as a Beatle, he recalled, he didn't need to do interviews or live appearances until he wanted to.

"Besides, I think you have to be a homosexual nowadays to succeed," he quipped. "I think the record companies are only catering for the 14-to-20 year old market and forget that older people like listening to music, too."

• The Deep Purple coup of getting Harrison on stage with them was just one of a series of incidents. In Perth, Ritchie Blackmore was almost punched out by Eric Clapton's bodyguard when he insisted on having a jam in his room with friends at one in the morning. In Auckland, the police chief commented that he had never seen so many criminal elements assemble in one point, when a mini-riot broke out at the band's concert. In Sydney, Jon Lord entertained patrons of an Italian restaurant he lunched in, with a selection of old piano classics.

— SIMON MAYNARD

but it still slips a tasty dose of classical sophistication into its repertoire."

It's clear that Jon Lord was happy to be back with Deep Purple, particularly in terms of how after his time with Whitesnake, he eventually went on to say that whilst with them, he felt that he had been somewhat reduced to the status of backing musician. A journalist commenting on Deep Purple's performance in Sydney said; "Whilst the rest of the band went off for a breather, Jon Lord launched into a stunning keyboard rave that ranged from snippets of Bach to Christmas carols." (They also commented that "Blackmore, although one of the most ferocious guitarists in the world, hushed the house with a lovely flamenco-inspired solo.")

One review stated that Deep Purple "proved last night at the [Sydney] Entertainment Centre, that despite ten years' absence, they can still play heavy metal music at its loudest and best... The players, dressed mainly in black, walked onto a smoke-filled stage for the first show of their Australian tour. They moved rapidly through a selection of songs from their new album, all of which received a good response, and one of their many classics, 'Strange Kind Of Woman'... The highlight of the show was probably 'Child In Time', a Deep Purple classic, with eerie undertones and dramatic build-up. With a strong use of keyboards, rapid drumbeat, and the superb guitar work of Ritchie Blackmore, Deep Purple managed to mesmerise the audience with almost every song. The superb lighting capped off a memorable night."

Calling the band "perhaps the greatest rock line-up of all time", a fan who saw them perform in Melbourne wrote to a local newspaper to say that they were "musically staggering", adding that Jon Lord "played a diversity of music in his solos, ranging from jazz to classical, through to amazing improvisations".

With the band's last date down under being in Melbourne

on the 18th December, they went home for Christmas for a few weeks off prior to the beginning of their American tour.

It's fascinating to consider that the reunion could have happened earlier. In late 1982, Mk2 had almost managed to get it together. A new album and some warm-up dates in South America had been discussed. The wheels were in motion in the background to the extent that a European promoter had earmarked potential venues for a supposed tour, and a Swedish newspaper printed in January 1983 went on to speculate on the possibility of a 1984 summer tour.

The latter was all speculation, of course, from those who were not privy to the inner workings of what was really happening (or not, as the case was). Still though, it shows that a) discussions of a reunion had been getting serious, and b) those who believed that it would happen there and then were certainly hungry for it.

Around this time, Blackmore and Glover were free to call it a day with Rainbow then. Jon Lord was still a member of Whitesnake but already had his eye on the exit. Ian Paice was with Gary Moore, but only in what was regarded as a "temporary permanent position".

Also around this time, Ian Gillan had been advised to take a six-month break from singing in order to save his throat from any permanent damage. He disbanded his Gillan band and was met by accusations from some members of having done so with an ulterior motive (what with how he went on to join Black Sabbath).

In 1983, Blackmore and Glover's dialogue with Gillan had even resulted in the trio going out for a meal to discuss the singer's idea for a reunion. Glover said; "We went to a restaurant for dinner and by the end of the meal, Ian was drunk. Ritchie and I decided then that we didn't want to deal with that."

Gillan gave a candid, but similar, account: "Drinking

doesn't actually pay off, because within ten minutes, Ritchie Blackmore and I told each other to fuck off and I ended up joining Black Sabbath for good money."

Regardless of what could have been for Deep Purple Mk2, it was very much a case of better late than never. Besides, having been given such a warm welcome in Australia, and with a string of good reviews to their credit, the band had everything to play for as 1984 came to a close.

Arrests at rock concert

AUCKLAND, Sun: More than 60 people were arrested after a bottle-wielding mob tried to overrun security guards at a rock concert given by the British group Deep Purple in Auckland tonight.

Violence erupted after people at the front of a crowd of about 1000, who were milling around the car park next to the open-air stadium, were turned away at the ticket barrier.

Bottles were thrown into the stadium entrance before police, wearing riot helmets and carrying batons, moved in to clear the crowd.

An Auckland promoter involved with the concert, Mr Patrick Connell, said that about 12,000 people had paid to hear Deep Purple.

There had been no trouble inside the stadium. – NZPA

A BIG BLUE FOR THE DEEP PURPLE

MORE than 60 people were arrested after a bottle-wielding mob clashed with riot police at a rock concert given by the British group Deep Purple at Auckland last night.

Violence erupted when people in a queue of 1000 were turned away at the ticket box because the open air stadium was full and they began throwing bottles into the entrance.

Deep Purple rocks back

DEEP Purple, rated the best of the British heavy metal bands in popularity and earnings before it split in 1973, will play Memorial Drive on Friday, November 30.

Bookings open at all Bass outlets for this rock phenomenon tomorrow.

Adelaide will see the revived band on its reunion world concert tour, taking in Australia, New Zealand and Japan.

The revived Deep Purple line-up (above), which has not performed together since 1972, consists of Ian Gillan, guitarist Ritchie Blackmore, Roger Glover on base, drummer Ian Paice and keyboard player Jon Lord.

Who Do We Think We Are

Concert: Deep Purple   **Venue:** Entertainment Centre

Deep Purple returns to relight the fire

Concert

By BRUCE GUTHRIE

British band Deep Purple first toured Australia about one thousand years ago, back in the early seventies.

It was then the world's heavy-metal heavyweight and beginning to look tired from bearing the burden.

The band played Festival Hall in 1971 in a triple bill which included other British outfits Manfred Mann's Earth Band and a fledgling Free, featuring Paul Rodgers. Deep Purple came in third despite being the headliner.

The band members played like they had nothing left to prove, but last night there was none of that seventies lethargy, even though each member is approaching middle age.

This was a Deep Purple reasserting itself and looking to the forefront of the current heavy-metal resurgence.

Of course the noise-levels haven't altered. The five-member band still plays LOUD. But unlike that early tour the musicians had some energy about them and moreover looked to be having lots of fun.

Last night's line-up was the one that took Deep Purple to its greatest heights: Ian Gillan, vocals, Ritchie Blackmore, guitar, Jon Lord, keyboards, Roger Glover, bass, and Ian Paice, drums.

Gillan and Glover left the band in 1973 and though replacements were tried, by 1975 Deep Purple was no more.

The band chose New Zealand and Australia as the first stops on its comeback trail.

Deep Purple was always the sum total of its parts, unlike other bands of the genre. While the interplay of Gillan, Blackmore and Lord provides the spark, it's only possible because of the foundation laid by Paice and Glover.

They started and finished the show with tracks from the seventies — a powerhouse Highway Star and a frenetic Speed King.

They will be back at the centre tonight and tomorrow to prove that not only can time sometimes stand still, it can sometimes be turned back.

Sydney's top gig guide   *Raging!*

A PURPLE EVENT IS ON WAY

Fans still remember

ROCK band Deep Purple — noted as being one of the loudest-playing outfits in the world — flew into Sydney and went straight to a press conference at Kings Cross.

The band still has a very strong following even though there were 11 years when members did their individual things. They recently re-formed the band.

Bass player Roger Glover is certain the band will go from strength to strength now the members are back together.

He said: "Our latest record, Perfect Stranger, sold 2 million copies in the first two weeks of release.

"So many people remember us and now we can sit back and say thanks a lot."

Drummer Ian Paice feared that the band would be criticised for reforming but was pleasantly surprised by the response of new and old fans.

"You can't analyse why it works or doesn't work but we enjoy it and a lot of people do too," he said.

Their Sydney concert is at the Entertainment Centre on December 13.

We've got 10 double passes to give away to the concert, along with 10 autographed copies of Deep Purple's album Perfect Strangers. See the coupon on this page.

— LEIGH REINHOLD

LOUD: Four of the five members of Deep Purple

Deep Purple hasn't lost its heavy metal touch

By TONY LIOCE
Journal-Bulletin Arts Writer

Music review

Deep Purple, heavy metal rock, Providence Civic Center, a Frank J. Russo production, last night and tonight.

PROVIDENCE — After 11 years apart, singer Ian Gillan, guitarist Ritchie Blackmore, keyboard player Jon Lord, bassman Roger Glover and drummer Ian Paice have reformed the British band Deep Purple. Their ads say "destiny" brought them back together. The truth probably has more to do with the failure of their solo careers.

Still, as they kicked off a two-night stand at the Civic Center last night, it was apparent that musically, they haven't lost much.

Never had much to begin with, you say? Well, it's true that Deep Purple will never go down in the same history books as the Stones, the Who, the Kinks and other more intelligent contemporaries. But one must admit that the band was influential (the heavy metal rockers who currently dominate the arena circuit have taken more than one cue from the work this group did in the old days) and beyond that, as bands of this stripe go, Deep Purple is a distinct cut above the pack.

Most heavy metal groups are nothing more than purveyors of aural sludge; Deep Purple's songs may be nothing to write home about, but last night the band played them with precision and even some passion.

THE RHYTHMS were relatively complex, Gillan's vocals amounted to something more than the foolish shouting to which listeners of heavy metal have become accustomed, and Blackmore — who always has been the band's star — proved he is still technically proficient and rather imaginative to boot.

Playing some new songs and many of its old hits, all at ear-splitting volume, Deep Purple lapsed more than occasionally into the self-indulgent egotism and pretentiousness that always attends heavy metal rock. But the band always seemed to bounce back.

Knocking At Your Back Door

January 1985 marked the first time that Deep Purple (the real one — not the fake Rod Evans one) were back on stage in America for the first time since 1976. It was the beginning of what would be a long tour covering major venues. The crowds lapped it up with full enthusiasm, as was demonstrative in the ticket sales.

The setlist was similar to that which had been used in Australia, but in anticipation of what American audiences would expect, the band reluctantly added 'Woman From Tokyo', which they performed on their opening night at Texas on the 24th.

'Knocking At Your Back Door' was released as a single in the US. The UK was given 'Perfect Strangers' with 'Son Of Alerik' (the ten-minute instrumental jam recorded as part of the *Perfect Strangers* album sessions) on the B-side.

Music Week reviewed 'Knocking At Your Back Door'; "Ageing rockers highlight the worst side of heavy metal with this dated, bombastic number complete with histrionic wailing. Limited edition twelve-inch version will no doubt appeal to nostalgic fans." It just goes to show that reviewers who weren't supportive of the reunion, really went to town with it on expressing their opinion.

Despite the fact that the UK single seemed to be welcomed by fans, the music press were less than supportive on that front too. *Melody Maker* called it "bland and sluggish" whilst *Music Week* called the band "old gits". It is worth noting here that by the mid-eighties, the music press was predominantly championing synth pop. Deep Purple's music was better supported by publications such as *Kerrang!* and *Metal Hammer*. It was in stark contrast to the seventies, where Deep Purple had been considered popular in the mainstream, and thus better supported by such media.

By February 1985, with the tour in full swing, Deep Purple were gaining momentum on stage, their sense of humour and improvisation becoming more apparent in their live performances. Although the solos were perhaps not as lengthy as they had been in the seventies, they were no less exciting, played with conviction and style.

Such was the demand for tickets, that in some cities, the authorities had to get involved. In St Louis, the police were required to intervene after a surge of fans had broken the doors of the booking office. Desperate to get tickets, the fans had been waiting in the snow for hours.

"It's very reassuring to us to see that the entire tour is sold out," Roger Glover said in February 1985. "Some of the bigger places — such as New York City, Los Angeles, Detroit, Philadelphia and Chicago — are selling very quickly. It is incredible really. We are putting in second shows in some areas. We are doing two shows in Chicago, three in New York, two in London, two in Los Angeles, and so on... We are just being bowled over by the enthusiasm. It feels just great. I would have never thought this would be happening again, the way that it is now. I suppose, there is something in the music this band makes that I have not found anywhere else."

The San Francisco Examiner reported in February 1985; "The return of Deep Purple, among the most abrasive and offensively loud rock bands of a decade ago, drew a large (but not capacity) crowd at the Cow Palace last night. Most in the

REVIEWS

Sat., Feb. 9, 1985, Denver

Deep Purple still hard-rocking

Deep Purple: Ritchie Blackmore, guitar; Ian Gillan, vocals; Jon Lord, keyboards; Roger Glover, bass, Ian Paice, drums. With: Giuffria at McNichols Arena.

By JUSTIN MITCHELL
Rocky Mountain News Staff Writer

Heavy metal, long the professional wrestling of rock and roll, regained some stature and respect with Deep Purple's reunion concert for about 14,000 *metalloids* at McNichols Arena on Friday night.

Though the show could have been an exercise in nostalgia or embarrassment, the band's five members (an incarnation from the early 1970s version of the band) proved to be innovative, entertaining and best of all, hard-rocking.

No Spandex, no S&M outfits and no hooded dwarfs worshiping 20-foot, fire-breathing, Egyptian vampires. Opening with the amphetamine-fast road riff "Highway Star" from the head-banging classic LP "Machine Head," the band went on to give the crowd generous portions of its past and present.

Much material was taken from Deep Purple's current album, "Perfect Strangers," the title track of which was spiced with a laser display and Jon Lord's classical-influenced organ solo. Other highlights from the album included the current single "Knocking at Your Back Door" and "The Gypsy's Kiss," which opened with a refreshing blues jam between guitarist Ritchie Blackmore, keyboardist Lord and vocalist Ian Gillian on congas.

Digging into their archives, the band went back to "Sweet Child in Time" from the "Deep Purple in Rock" album recorded in 1970. A slide reproduction of the LP was shown on a screen behind the group, perhaps to remind those in attendance who might not have been born when the record was released. It was at this point that Gillian really unleashed his vocal chops. Aided with an echo/delay system, he went from plaintive to paranoid with a voice that could dice, slice chop and puree rodents at 300 feet.

It wasn't all histrionics, though. Beethoven's "Ode to Joy" received a heavy-metal baptism, courtesy of Messrs. Blackmore and Lord. The adaptation was crowned with a laser-animated projection of Beethoven conducting the boys.

The opening band Giuffria was everything Deep Purple wasn't. Fronted by lead singer David Glen Eisley, the band was long on codpieces, Spandex tights while posturing and short on talent. They even make Journey, their apparent role model, sound good. And that's bad.

rather young audience came to hear the group because 'you know, they're legends', as one young man told me... Deep Purple seemed unbearably loud a dozen years ago, but last night the band's sounds were well-balanced, rich and deep. Only Blackmore's guitar occasionally grated the eardrums. The keyboards were, if anything, not loud enough. Gillan's vocals seem a bit dated now, especially the histrionic falsetto endings, but otherwise last night's show was a comfortable blend of old and new — both in music and technology. The ninety-minute performance drew from the current LP, *Perfect Strangers*, as well as a number of the early seventies' albums, and the production featured an effective laser-beam show as well as the usual spotlights and backdrop projections. Most of the time, the rear projection was a reproduction of the 1970 *Deep Purple In Rock* album cover, the quintet seemingly chiselled in stone à la Mount Rushmore. From the current LP, 'Knocking At Your Back Door', 'Perfect Strangers', 'Under The Gun', and the bluesy 'A Gypsy's Kiss', were remarkably effective; the Deep Purple cohesion is better than ever. The arrangements are far more sophisticated than those used by contemporary young heavy metal groups who listen to Deep Purple for inspiration."

"Gillan's habit of singing a chorus, leaving the stage, returning to play conga drums, leaving again, then returning to sing some more, is strange to young rock fans, but familiar to those who followed the heavier metal bands of yesteryear. Although each member of the band had a chance for some featured solo work, happily all was rather short. It was the full-throated ensemble work that distinguished Deep Purple last night, as it did in the seventies. Some might find the older Deep Purple material, with its piano and guitar (or organ and guitar) flourishes, a bit pompous, but last night, mixed with modern Deep Purple stuff, it came off very well."

Under the heading of "Deep Purple Reunited And It

Sounds So Good", *The Pittsburgh Press* reported in February 1985; "The house lights went off, and the lighters were held aloft. Laser light patterns rotated on a large backdrop screen, finally resolving themselves into a large "DP". The musicians sauntered silently on stage. The fans howled their approval. There was no introduction. None was needed. This was Deep Purple. More important, it was the five-man line-up that made Deep Purple one of the first superstar heavy metal bands, and that hadn't played here since 31st May 1973. And last night at the Civic Arena, Ian Gillan, Ritchie Blackmore, Jon Lord, Roger Glover and Ian Paice proved to a sell-out crowd of 13,617 (seats behind the stage weren't put on sale) that heavy metal not only is alive and well, but it doesn't have to be mindless and/or pandering as so much of it has become."

"In many ways, this extra-loud concert was just like that evening almost a dozen years ago when most of last night's fans were in grade school or even preschool. Gillan, in far better voice than on his solo albums after leaving Deep Purple in '73, often forsook singing to tear the roof off with his shrieks. Lord stuck mainly to his Hammond organ, although he added a few synthesisers. Bassist Glover and drummer Paice provided a rock-solid foundation, and the latter hasn't trimmed his mutton chops. Blackmore, who played here several times with Rainbow after quitting Deep Purple shortly after Gillan did, sometimes lets the notes cascade out of his guitar in a jumbled maelstrom and sometimes was more reserved and tasteful, as on 'Knocking At Your Back Door'. In either case, the notes emerged almost effortlessly. And there were plenty of old favourite numbers, starting with set-opener 'Highway Star' and continuing with bouncier, bluesier 'Strange Kind Of Woman', 'Child In Time', 'Speed King' (just what the title suggests), 'Space Truckin'', a snippet of 'Woman From Tokyo' and an inspired rendition of 'Smoke On The Water', complete with sing-along choruses, to close the almost two-hour set."

"In other ways, however, it was quite different. Deep Purple was not, as Glover said, 'an oldies band on an oldies tour'. They had plenty of new material, led by an excellent, extended concert version of 'Knocking At Your Back Door'. Sinister-sounding 'Perfect Strangers' wasn't far behind. What kept these slam-it-out songs from being mindless? Gillan, when he decided to sing instead of shriek. Blackmore in his less frantic moments. Lord's seasonings. Melodies. Intelligent, imaginative lyrics like 'Smoke On The Water's, autobiographical ones. That isn't to say, though, that Deep Purple was perfect. After 'Perfect Strangers', and after treating the fans to a show that included vertical bars of lights on the screen and green laser lights at the edge of the stage, at stage left and right and behind Gillan, they simply walked off for about five minutes."

"People vote for more. Nothing. The cheers turned to boos. Nothing. Finally, Deep Purple returned. No explanation. No nothing. And after that, Deep Purple, although continuing to mix old and new songs adroitly and continuing to sport such stunning visual effects as a red, white and black spiral design, and a laser light drawing of Beethoven's face, and of Beethoven "conducting" them, often turned needlessly self-indulgent. Blackmore fiddled and faddled through part of old Ludwig's Ninth Symphony. Lord did the same, switching from classical to jazz to boogie-woogie to ragtime. 'Space Truckin'' and 'Speed King' were dragged on and on with still more unnecessary racket. Perhaps it was just the joy of being reunited, having an album that's doing well, and knowing they're cultivating a new crop of fans that made Deep Purple go off the deep end too often. But with so many good songs left undone ('Stormbringer', 'Lazy' and even 'Hush', for instance), it wasn't becoming to a band that should have known better and otherwise did such a good job."

Of course, there was no way that any audience, no matter how hungry for it, was going to get a rendition of 'Stormbringer'. "I actually to this day have never heard, nor do I possess, *Burn* or *Stormbringer* or anything since," Gillan told a journalist. "All I know is that riff to 'Burn'. I don't know the song, I don't know the tempo. I don't have an idea — and for the simple reason that I saw my lover with someone else, and I couldn't bring myself to even contemplate the possibility. It was such a deeply emotional thing that I didn't want to hear. So I haven't even heard it to this day. I think on one or two occasions, I've gone completely out of my way to avoid hearing it. I mean, if it's on the radio, I'd walk out of the room or turn it off. Not because I had any bad feelings for David or anything like that. I just didn't want to know."

Fortunately for Gillan, fan demand for the 1970s Mk2 material was alive and well. In March 1985, EMI released picture discs of the classic Purple albums, *In Rock*, *Fireball* and *Machine Head*. With Edwards and Coletta and HEC Enterprises owning the original recordings, they were free to exploit the newfound interest in Deep Purple. In fact, interest had never gone away. In 1980, HEC had released a compilation, *Deepest Purple*, which hit the number one spot in the UK. This was followed by a double album, *In Concert*, at the end of that year. It combined two BBC performances from 1970 and 1972. Two years later, *Live In London* was released. Another BBC recording, this time from 1974, it featured the Mk3 line-up.

There were some occasions where Blackmore declined to do 'Smoke On The Water' as part of the encore, instead opting to go to his dressing room. One such instance of this was on 25th March when the band played at Brendan Byrne Arena, The Meadowlands, New Jersey.

Under the heading of "'Smoke'-less Deep Purple Retreats To The Stone Age", New Jersey's *The Courier News* reported;

"They didn't play 'Smoke On The Water'. What Deep Purple did present during their sold-out concert at the Brendan Byrne Arena last night was a rather Dickensian show, recalling the best of their times and the worst excesses of hard rock. Jon Lord heralded the band's entrance shortly after 8:30pm with a loud Hammond organ rendition of the *Phantom Of The Opera* theme [actually Bach's Toccata in D Minor]. As the veteran keyboardist built to a crescendo, two flash pots exploded and Deep Purple kicked into the classic 'Highway Star'. It took the better part of the opening number for the PA to be properly adjusted, with 'Highway Star' consequently lost in the aural mud. But after the initial problem, the sound was clear and at a reasonable volume, surprising since Deep Purple had once been known as one of the loudest bands in the world."

"The welcome accorded Deep Purple after the opening number was one of the loudest heard in the arena since the Springsteen summer concerts. Lead vocalist Ian Gillan seemed truly moved by the ovation, repeatedly thanking the crowd. As they ran through some of the earlier material, Deep Purple showed why they were one of rock's most beloved bands in the early seventies, blending snippets of classical music into their solos and using dynamics to a degree unheard of among today's younger arena rock stars. On 'Strange Kind Of Woman', guitarist Ritchie Blackmore showed that his usually dour stage persona has a lighter side, and he threw in short quotes from *Jesus Christ Superstar* and 'Jesu, Joy Of Man's Desiring' into his long solo."

"Unfortunately, the subtle side Deep Purple showed early in the evening soon deteriorated into a noisy amalgam of feedback and overly-long solos, bringing back unpleasant memories of the "dinosaur rock" era that was kicked in the pants by punk bands like The Ramones in the late seventies. Near the end of the two-hour concert, the audience was listless, almost groaning audibly as another endless solo was launched. Following a lively version of 'Space Truckin'' to close the regular programme, Deep Purple returned after a long pause with 'Woman From Tokyo' as three huge coloured balloons were bounced about by the crowd."

By April 1985, the American leg of the tour came to an end. It had been a roaring success, with halls all sold out. Often ticket resellers were able to make quite the profit, with fans desperate to get into a venue at the last minute.

With Deep Purple taking four weeks off before taking the tour to Japan, demand for the band was accommodated by bootleggers. *Back In Action* was most likely the first of many (which is, of course, difficult to confirm due to the nature of bootlegging and its lack of official cataloguing). Around this time, the bulk of material on bootlegs seemed to have been sourced from cassette recordings of the Australian shows. They were particularly popular in Europe, with fans keen to hear what the band sounded like live by this point.

In May 1985, Deep Purple performed a total of seven shows in Japan, with four at the Budokan in Tokyo. Although no official recording was made, a bootleg — *The Perfect Stranger* — was circulated thereafter.

Following another four-week break, Deep Purple were back in Europe for the first time in almost ten years. There were not nearly enough shows put on to reach the number of fans who were keen to support them. Europe was given just sixteen shows over the course of four weeks, and only one of those was in Britain. During this time, the setlist remained the same as it had done in Australia. However, there were some gigs during which 'Child In Time' was left out when Gillan didn't feel up to it.

To coincide with the European dates (and in particular, the band's return to UK soil), in conjunction with HEC, EMI released *The Anthology*. A double album of material from 1968-76, it included three previously unheard recordings. Did such releases add to the band's then-current status, or diminish it?

Still though, the show in Britain was a large-scale one, and monumental at that! The reviews of Deep Purple's performance at Knebworth on Saturday 22nd June were pretty mixed, as were the reviews of Knebworth overall, in fact. Unsurprising really, considering a) the nature of festivals, and b) the terrible weather. For some, Deep Purple were the main attraction within an exuberant and youthful atmosphere, whilst others had probably just had enough and wanted to go home! Everyone's experience — and perceptions — of Knebworth were clearly different, as is evidenced by the significant variation in each journalist's estimation of the number in attendance.

The *Birmingham Evening Mail* considered; "Status at rock festivals shows itself in the number of dressing rooms you have. The bigger you are, the more portable cabins you get. Thus at Knebworth Fayre, Alaska, Mountain, Mama's Boys and Blackfoot had a cabinet apiece. Meat Loaf, UFO and Scorpions merited two, and Deep Purple had seven. More than 70,000 fans paid fourteen pounds each to see Purple's first comeback show on British soil — or mud to be precise. Torrential rainfall turned Knebworth's pastures into a quagmire, and the weather — kind only to the opening bands — turned from bad to worse. Coachloads of fans travelled from the Midlands and the adverse conditions served only to instil a manic determination to enjoy the day at any cost. That was probably a good thing. Deep Purple, like their dressing rooms, were cluttered, undisciplined, and self-indulgent."

"Ian Gillan, Ritchie Blackmore, Jon Lord, Roger Glover and Ian Paice failed to recapture the old glory, shaking, not stirring. They were only fair at the Fayre. Only Glover and Paice escaped bouts of musical flatulence. Midlander Lord was good, but predictable as the weather, and Gillan and Blackmore were parodies of their former selves. Gillan screeched where he used to soar, and Blackmore's interminable solos were played for, rather than with, effect. The fireworks came after — not during — the set. Purple played adequately, but even classics like 'Strange Kind Of Woman' and 'Woman From Tokyo' failed to get the adrenaline running. Sodden fans were already leaving well before 'Smoke On The Water'."

"Plans to make this the loudest rock show ever were scuppered by the local council, but Alaska, Mama's Boys and Meat Loaf turned in short, effective sets. UFO and Scorpions were brash and lively, and Mountain were monumentally boring. Surprises of the day were Blackfoot, who showed genuine attack and enthusiasm. It's something I hope Purple rediscover. They used to be one of the truly great live bands, and — let's be honest — tens of thousands of fans at Knebworth still thought they were. The return of Deep Purple? Deeply disappointing."

From *The Daily Mail* (under the heading of "Deep Purple Saved The Muddy Fayre"); "Deep Purple, one of the finest rock bands ever, reunited last year to the delight of their legions of fans worldwide. Last weekend, the British band returned to home soil after many years away. It was a triumphant return to Britain — and they saved the special Knebworth Fayre from disappearing into the mud. Before their breath-taking appearance, the most notable feature of the day had been the pitched battle between various factions of the 60,000-strong crowd, who preferred to engage in hurling bottles and mud rather than watch the bands. Mind you, at times, the traditional open-air "war" proved far more entertaining than the stereotype thrash bands which strutted about the stage. Bernie Marsden's Alaska left the crowd cold, Mountain have slipped from their peak, and the group Mama's Boys looked and sounded exactly that. Blackfoot occasionally grabbed the crowd's attention with their brand of Deep South

R&B, but the biggest cheer of their set resulted from one of the band being clouted in the face by a bottle. Phil Mogg's UFO were greeted generously by the crowd, but once again the mudslinging started, and even a memorable encore of 'Doctor Doctor' proved no remedy."

"As the first of the heavyweights hobbled on to the stage, the audience began to settle down, but Meat Loaf disappointed. His voice doesn't have the same power as on records and the piano-dominated backing music made some of the numbers sound like entries for the Eurovision Song Contest. German band the Scorpions were a welcome change. Rather than weakly asking the crowd to stop throwing projectiles, they assailed their eardrums and forced them to rock and roll. Their performance was immaculate. The music and singing combined faultlessly and the group's acrobatics gave their act that something different. I look forward to the next British tour."

"So to the main event — preceded by desperate pleas from DJ Tommy Vance to stop throwing things onto the stage. All well and good, but he didn't have to stand for one-and-a-half hours in the pouring rain while the set was changed. Still, all that was forgotten as the opening strains of 'Highway Star' rang out when the band appeared in a frame of blinding white light. Complemented by an excellent laser and lighting display, the band gave an unforgettable performance, with Gillan shining through on vocals. At times, some of the crowd seemed to feel the solos went on too long, but that is what Deep Purple are about; every performer a star in his own right. In the decades that the group split, each of the members have tasted success in other bands, and this led to the belief that the reunion was strictly for fun rather than money. That's certainly the way it came across. The band were called back five times and every number deserves a mention. 'Black Night' was particularly memorable. Finally, as Roger Glover and Ritchie

Blackmore thumped out the opening strains of 'Smoke On The Water', the crowd reacted as one. Gillan wasn't needed. The reaction was phenomenal. Deep Purple showed no sign of ageing, and saved the day at Knebworth. Let's hope that if they appear next year, they will be more ably supported."

From the *Hertfordshire Mercury And County Press*; "Appalling weather turned Saturday's big Knebworth music festival into a mud bath. Some 65,000 people converged on Knebworth Park for the all-day heavy metal bonanza. By the time the crowds disappeared, the grounds of the stately Hertfordshire house looked like a quagmire. A number of tractors had been strategically placed by the organisers, and the police spent hours in the rain rescuing motorists and coaches stuck in the mud. Inspector Christopher Partridge, police press officer at Welwyn Garden City, said there was only one arrest in the park and eleven in the vicinity. 'The day was remarkably problem-free. The main trouble was vehicles stuck in the mud. It was dreadful, as it had been raining consistently from four, to eight or nine pm,' he added. Amazingly, there was a break in the downpour soon after main act Deep Purple started playing, and it stayed fine for a spectacular fireworks display, which ensured the group's last number went off with a bang. Financially, the day was a dead loss for promoter Paul Loasby, considering the amount of work he had put into the festival — the largest Knebworth for five years. But he maintained that artistically, the show had been worthwhile. Herts Red Cross and the St John Ambulance brigade treated some three-hundred casualties throughout the day. Injuries included a fractured leg, burns, and some cuts which needed stitches. Five people were taken to hospital after bottles had been thrown."

Blackmore wore wellies for the whole set, and due to the lack of suitable roofing against the rain, Lord's equipment remained covered in polythene for the whole performance. A few years after the festival, the keyboardist empathised with the crowd, saying that "they all got soaked, poor people. I felt sorry for them all sitting in the mud".

"At the risk of annoying the rest of the band, I'd say I personally thought just playing at Knebworth was a bad decision," he added. "I can't really remember why that decision was made. It just seemed like a good idea at the time. I'm being honest. I do remember voicing my opinion at the time — as did Ian Gillan, *very* strongly — but the others were ambivalent: 'Oh, it's right in the middle of the summer, it'll be a great occasion, it will be a beautiful day'. Ha ha ha! Mudworth! Do you know that was the wettest summer solstice in the history of record keeping?!"

Sadly, the BBC recorded more audio than visual footage of Deep Purple's performance at Knebworth. Gillan, Glover and Lord were briefly interviewed together for a local news broadcast, and a tiny segment of 'Highway Star' was included, but that was it. Around forty minutes of the band's set was broadcast on BBC Radio One the following weekend.

Prior to doing Knebworth, Blackmore was asked about why the band weren't doing more British dates. His answer: "We took kind of a vote. Some of the band wanted to do more gigs, and some wanted to do one big one. But it's so difficult — when you've got a big production — to break even when you play in England, which is why not too many bands go there. I wanted to do a few gigs — one in Scotland, one in Birmingham, two in London, something like that, but I was overruled by someone. I can't remember who, someone I met in a pub somewhere I expect. I don't like to be judged on one gig because it's inevitably a disappointment, everything goes wrong. I could say the halls in Britain aren't big enough, but I really don't know the answers. I can just see people saying now, 'Oh the halls aren't big enough to hold Ritchie's head!' I know if it was down to Ian Gillan, the band would do every club and hall in Britain, but I don't know, politics come into play, and all kinds of things, and it's ended up that the band is doing a European tour with three days off before Knebworth, and three days off after, so we probably could have done something more. I think it's got to the point where I can't even remember the real reasons we're not doing a British tour. We're gonna kick off the European tour by playing a small club date in Sweden, actually. Just invite members of the fan club, and do it secretly so the promoter doesn't start charging people a fortune to see it."

In July, the band's two shows in Paris were filmed by the German TV company, WDR. The second night was broadcasted as part of the *Rockpalast* series. The footage wasn't given an official commercial release at the time — possibly owing to the fact that Gillan was clearly struggling that night with a heavy cold. The first night's performance also had its problems; Lord's Hammond stopped working during 'Space Truckin'' and he had to continue that number, and the encore, on piano.

Also that month, Deep Purple played at an all-day open-air festival in Germany. Without the extreme weather conditions of Knebworth, the band and the fans could embrace the music, although some fan accounts stipulate that Gillan was struggling vocally at these performances too.

To allow Gillan's voice to rest, two dates that had been booked for Spain (Madrid on 2nd, and Barcelona on 3rd July) were rescheduled for two weeks later (to Barcelona on 16th, and Madrid on 17th). They were the last shows of the European tour.

In August, the first reunion tour wrapped up in America. The last date was at the Texas World Music Festival, where Deep Purple performed to a crowd of around over 60,000 people. As the headlining act, the band came on stage around eight hours into the event.

Such was the crowd-drawing power of Deep Purple, that for the organiser of the Texas World Music Festival, the band's presence was the difference between whether or not to run the event. "It has been something of a struggle putting together the right combination of talent and I had decided not to do the show this year," they said. "But I was eventually convinced to do it, and getting Deep Purple as headliner certainly was a major factor. That had a lot to do with my decision to go ahead. In my opinion, Deep Purple is the success story of the year. They certainly were the surprise of the year. Here's a band that hadn't been together in their current form for more than ten years. Yet they were able to come back stronger than ever."

With the tour all wrapped up, it was time for Ian Gillan to have his tonsils removed. The rest and relaxation that followed was much needed. According to Glover, they had "already agreed that because of what happened in the early days, we would give each other plenty of time to get away from each other. The idea was to take six months off and then get together to do an album".

Billboard later went on to report that Deep Purple had been the biggest grossing live act of the year. The reunion had been a tremendous success — and then some!

"The reunion exceeded all our expectations," said Gillan. "It was something all five of us very much wanted, but of course, we didn't know how the public would react. *Perfect Strangers* was a very spontaneous thing. We were full of ideas and before we knew what was going on, the album was finished. When we went back on stage after such a long time, it was just great."

"I couldn't believe the business we did and the amount of records we sold," Blackmore said. "We had to double-up everywhere we went — Australia, Germany, America — and I was worried about filling out one show in each city; in fact, we ended up doing two sold-out nights everywhere. It's nice to know that so many people wanted to come along to the shows. Deep down inside, I'm a very cynical person and I always think no one's going to show up, no one's interested. That's why I shy away from interviews, because I can be very negative, and I don't want to represent the band in a negative way."

"This tour has been amazing," Glover said. "It's fulfilling all kinds of wishes, and certainly more than anything we ever anticipated. The audiences are a lot younger than we thought they'd be, and that again is reassuring — the fact that we were successful to one generation and now seem to be just as successful to the next generation."

That's not to say that Deep Purple's audience weren't a diverse bunch though! "You can see people sitting back there nodding quietly," said Lord. "You know they're the older fans, the ones with the worn-out copies of *Deep Purple In Rock* at home."

"We knew there would be some interest," Glover said. "After all, we've often been credited with having started the so-called heavy rock trend with albums like *Deep Purple In Rock* and *Made In Japan*. And radio has never stopped playing songs like 'Smoke On The Water' and 'Highway Star', even though Deep Purple completely ceased to be in 1976. But never in a million years did we expect this. It seems like we're now bigger than ever before."

In October 1985, Tommy Vance aired a Knebworth special on his radio show. Roger Glover turned his production talents to mixing some old Rainbow tapes for the forthcoming retrospective album, *Finyl Vinyl*. Overall, by the end of 1985, things were quiet on the Purple front. Despite the full intention to work on a new album, it wouldn't be until well into 1986 — a year of no tours for them — that the band would next get together in the studio.

Perfect Strangers - *Deep Purple 1984-1993*

Deep Purple back with a vengeance

DEEP PURPLE – In concert with Girlschool at the Worcester Centrum, Thursday night.

By Ernie Welch
Special to The Globe

MUSIC REVIEW

WORCESTER – Why the Mark II version of England's Deep Purple, disbanded since 1973, has been selling out major venues across the States can be answered in three words: "Made in Japan." A live double album recorded in the Land of the Rising Sun in 1972, "Made In Japan" documents nonpareil power rock – monster music that picks you up and simply blows you away.

Thursday at the first of three Centrum shows (tonight and tomorrow follow), Deep Purple surprised skeptics and lavished on loyalists a two-hour, streamlined feast for the senses that may be remembered as "Made in Worcester." It was that good.

Complemented by a tasteful array of visual effects and an austere assortment of cube-shaped props, Purple hit the launching pad burnin' and jettisoned the crowd with "Highway Star," channeling pleasures of the flesh, mind and spirit in one metaphysical rush.

"Nobody's Home," a contemporarily compact tune from the new "Perfect Strangers" album, slowed the pace a bit. But the band hit passing gear again with "Strange Kind of Woman." Ritchie Blackmore's initial exploration into the land of impossible guitar. Snatching snippets from the theme to "Jesus Christ Superstar," Blackmore's solo traveled somewhere between progressive blues and martian boogie before it veered into a nimble call-and-response with vocalist Ian Gillan, which was cleverly picked up by organist Jon Lord who kicked in the coda.

Relying on stunning, synchronized lighting and pure chops, Purple expressed visceral and instrumental power without resorting to phony emotional outbursts and visual exaggerations. Instead of carrying on like so many oversexed yahoos fronting similar bands, Gillan addressed the audience as an educated English gentleman with working class grit. His strong, soaring voice was amazing, particularly when his wails seemed to reach heaven during "Child In Time." And when he cooked on the conga drums, Gillan looked like the Desi Arnaz Lucille Ball never knew.

Lord, Blackmore, drummer Ian Paice and bassist Roger Glover were also models of confident restraint. They certainly have egos – one backdrop was an enlargement of an album cover where the Mt. Rushmore faces are substituted with the band's – but each let the music do the talking. Paice, a master at shifting the beat, transition fills and speed rolls, didn't make a V with his sticks or stand on his stool. Lord usually sat at his keyboards, though he did shake his Hammond B-3 organ in two solo breaks as he merged Bachesque cathedral flourishes with a rocket piano boogie. And when Blackmore rolled over Beethoven – while a computerized image of a classical conductor clapped and danced in the background – he played with cool control, leaving the masturbatory moves to the posers and young upstarts.

Blazing their way through such classics as "Lazy," "Woman From Tokyo," and 'Smoke On The Water," and a few new gems (the Led Zeppelinesque elephant walk, "Perfect Strangers" crushed the house), Deep Purple returned from the past with a sound that should insure a solid future. It's doubtful that anyone left the Centrum disappointed.

A last-minute replacement for Giuffria, Girlschool opened with a sizzling set of table turnin' crush rock. Strengthened by the additional firepower of new lead guitarist Cris Bonnacci and vocalist Jackie Bodimeadk, Girlschool is

Deep Purple Displays Heavy Mettle

By ROY NILSON

Buy stock in a hearing-aid company. Plug your ears with cotton. More than 10,000 people went deaf in the Centrum last night and another 20,000 or so will expose themselves to the same punishment Saturday and Sunday nights.

The Guinness Book of World Records once listed Deep Purple under the category "Loudest," and this reunion band still deserves the honor, if honor it was.

The trouble is that even 75 or so four-by-four speaker cabinets have trouble generating as much sound as Deep Purple demands. The human ear can only take so much for so long. Standing in the middle of a massive explosion, even a finely tuned explosion, for two hours can get boring unless the blastmasters take great care to spike the thunder with more than an occasional flash of lightning.

Back After 10-Year Hiatus

Deep Purple put its act back together after a 10-year hiatus and came out on the road this year to play the songs that created the brand of rock 'n' roll called "heavy metal." They came out to prove that metal music can be interesting, that rock 'n' roll is aging, but that even aging rockers can have fun. You know what? Deep Purple is right, even if they are asking more of speakers than speakers can deliver — even if the band insists on playing at magnum-force, megasonic, flesh compressing, brain-flattening volumes. Even an emergency medical technician, outside the hall and in a room facing away from the music, was wearing ear plugs last night.

About the Players

Ian Gillan was in good voice and good humor as Deep Purple opened with *Highway Star*. Ian Paice is more than equal to the task of making drums sound like rolling cannon fire. Roger Glover is content to thunder with his bass. He's waiting for one of the best bass lines ever written — but Deep Purple is saving *Smoke on the Water* for the last.

Nobody's Home comes close to syncopated assault and battery from the Jon Lord keyboard.

Ritchie Blackmore can deliver girder-flexing shrieks from his lead guitar, but he is capable of beautiful economies of melody and he slides those into *Strange Kind of Woman*.

Besides loud, heavy metal has a reputation for being repetitious. But Blackmore refused the stereotype several times last night and offered a pure blues introduction to *Gypsy's Kiss*.

Purple's members have created bands that depended on elaborate stage creations to make their way, but for this tour Deep Purple has rediscovered visual simplicity and let great racks of lighting provide the color on a stage set only with speaker boxes and backed by a featureless fabric screen.

About the Audience

Out in the audience, fans that were toddling when Deep Purple cut its first record contract mingled with fans who haven't dressed up in jeans or concert tour shirts for 15 years. The louder the volume, the more the fans screamed, though some took intermittent refuge from the noise out in the concourse.

The brand new *Perfect Strangers*, or *Perfect St. Rangers*, as Gillan called it, stands up well to a full-house concert treatment, even though Lord stuck in a lengthy keyboard solo that didn't measure up to his full strength. Another long solo, this one from Blackmore in the middle of *Under the Gun*, kept things slowing down.

Blackmore, Lord and Glover brought the action back with a duet of dangerous stops and starts in *Lazy* — but their timing was flawless. Glover tossed a fine bass line into *Child In Time* and Gillan spiced things up with *Knocking at Your Back Door*.

Basal Metabolism, Anyone?

If there was anyone left in the hall whose metabolism still was running at idle, he was buried under the floor a century before the Centrum was put up.

Lord inserted *Beethoven*, an instrumental tribute to several hundred years of music, into the program. Imagine a madman phantom of the opera pulling out all the stops on the biggest organ ever made — and playing strains from the *Ode to Joy*. He change the piece into a page or two of free-form piano work, turned a phrase of "Yankee Doodle Went to Town" into sheer honkytonk blues and slid in a line from the the theme from *2001: A Space Odyssey*. Only then did he allow the piece to slide into *Space Trucking*.

The Encores

An encore of *My Woman From Tokyo* was fast becoming the best part of the show when Gillam cut it off before it was done halfway and started introducing the band. A second encore, of *Speed King*, turned into a chest-crushing cantata for keyboard and guitar before Gillam led Deep Purple into *Smoke on the Water*, the song made for the bass guitar. Glover was sailing when Gillam chilled the middle of the work by calling for a sing-along. The audience was too weak to help out, but Deep Purple staged a major recovery and laid a great finish into the song before calling it a night and heading for the dressing room.

The all-female band *Schoolgirl* opened for Deep Purple and seemed intent on proving that even reasonably competent rockers can fall into the heavy metal all-alike sound that leads straight to boredom. Gil Weston-Jones plays a laconic bass. Jackie Bodimead can deliver a heavy-metal lyric and Cris Bonacci plays an adequate lead guitar. But the act lacks magic

The Gazette Reviews
ROCK

Perfect Strangers - *Deep Purple 1984-1993*

Deep Purple blasts back to wow

Rock

John Wendeborn

Deep Purple
Playing at.................. Memorial Coliseum

Deep Purple has returned to the rock wars with all the chutzpah of a chainsaw in heat.

After a layoff of a dozen years to perhaps do some R&R in their English countryside estates, the classic version of the Deep Purple quintet — Ritchie Blackmore, Ian Paice, Ian Gillan, Roger Glover and Jon Lord — is back doing what it does best: heavy metal with a snarl.

In a field of rock populated mostly these days by youths half their age, these five Britons held their own Monday night in Memorial Coliseum for several thousand young fans. It was reminiscent of the band's shows in the early '70s, except the coliseum was not even close to being sold out.

There's still enough fire in their old bones to melt iron here, though. They may be somewhere in their late 30s or early 40s, but cavorting onstage in front of a howling audience actually knows no age barriers.

Some of the music was far too dissonant, turning to loud dust under the alternately mellow and caterwauling voice of Gillan. Yet some of it truly simmered and turned into seething rave-ups of what this music is all about: Power, power, power.

Purple headbangers are true to their "school," however, and every song was greeted with affectionate enthusiasm. That many in the crowd weren't old enough to have heard Purple the first time around makes little difference. The band's reputation precedes it, and metalmongers know a good thing when they hear it.

Blackmore's usually sonorous guitar work made up several highlights, but when he turned to showboating via sound effects, it turned into a sour mash of noise. But when that beautifully soaring Blackmore guitar did sing, it proved again that few are in his league.

Lord's work on keyboards was astonishing. He didn't drift off into nothingness — ever. On the Beethoven "Ode To Joy," a spectacular Purple "suite" of rock sounds augmented by a laser cartoon of Beethoven "conducting" the band, Lord was at his best.

The nearly two-hour show included a lot of old Purple material, making it something of a nostalgia show at times. "Smoke On the Water" was the biggest nostalgic winner of the evening.

Girlschool opened the concert.

Nobody's Home

With fans still hungry for their Purple, more bootlegs were released. On the official front, the first quarter of 1986 was a quiet period for the band. During this time, even the musicians from other Deep Purple line-ups weren't up to much. Whitesnake was still paused whilst Coverdale spent some time thinking about which direction to take his band in, which included the search for new talent.

Much to the surprise of many people though, the rumours that Glenn Hughes had joined Black Sabbath turned out to be true. His recording with the band was fruitful, with *Seventh Star*. It was in essence a Tony Iommi solo album, but pressure from the record company saw it being marketed as Black Sabbath featuring Tony Iommi. Sadly for Hughes, the supporting tour — simply billed as Black Sabbath — was a disaster. His drug dependency deeply affected his performances and after just five shows in March '87, he was replaced by Ray Gillen.

Anyone in search of their Rainbow fix was in for a treat, with *Finyl Vinyl* — a double compilation — being released in March 1986.

It was on 12th April that Deep Purple finally got to work on what would become *The House Of Blue Light*. They had originally considered Massachusetts, but then decided to go back to Stowe, Vermont. Gillan had spent some time at Glover's house in Greenwich, Connecticut, writing material prior to getting into the studio to record.

Plans of recording *The House Of Blue Light* at Long

View Farm Studios in Central Massachusetts — where the Rolling Stones had rehearsed in 1981 — had to be scrapped when the band were unable to find enough accommodation for their families. Stowe was proud to host Deep Purple; a plaque commemorating their stay was hung on the wall of an English-owned pub they frequented ("We didn't do any damage there," said Gillan. "We just partied hard.").

Jon Lord said of Vermont; "It's a super part of the world. Far enough away from the city to avoid temptations, but close to a town with a couple of bars and nice restaurants, so you can get out and relax for a while. It's a fabulous place for us to go."

The album was produced by Roger Glover with Nick Blagona responsible for the engineering. In late September, Glover mixed the album at Union Studios in Munich. Although the whole band was supposed to be present, people came and went as required, mostly to do the occasional overdub.

There were rumours in circulation that America could expect to see the album released in late October, but it wasn't to be. During this period, the possibility that the album would be titled Black & White — as per one of the tracks — had been discussed.

"The title, *The House Of Blue Light*, is taken from the song 'Speed King' on our *In Rock* album," said Gillan. "We thought it sounded right, and it gave us a good idea for the cover. It was the only title all five of us like."

Not only did the album's title pay homage to the lyric used in 'Speed King'. The lyric was originally written in reference to Little Richard's 'Good Golly, Miss Molly', the line in itself having been taken from the 1946 song 'The House Of Blue Lights' composed by Don Raye and Freddie Slack. It had been a hit by Chuck Miller in 1955, and was also recorded by Chuck Berry — the same year (1958) that Little Richard scored a hit with 'Good Golly, Miss Molly'!

Blackmore said that a lot of material for the final mix had to be re-recorded, which is potentially a possibility as to why the album came to market later than had been anticipated. Polygram didn't receive test pressings until 18th December, and so consequently, had no choice but to move the release date to January 1987.

When it came to review time, although some were highly disparaging of Deep Purple's 1987 album, there were some who spoke very highly of it; no matter what was going on for the band behind the scenes, and despite how much the album was despised by some, it certainly wasn't without its musical merit to and bad reviews were not unanimous. It just goes to show that the narrative accumulated with hindsight does not necessarily mirror the entirety of what was said about the album (and how it was received) at the time.

Notably, it got to number thirty-four in the US, and to number ten in the UK. It also ranked within the top ten in several other European countries, and in Japan as well.

Kerrang! was amongst those who had been invited to preview the album prior to its release. They said: "I'd actually arrived in Montreux the night before, and had already been treated to a playback of the new Purple album, along with a number of other foreign journalists in a nearby casino. Six of the ten tracks you can expect to find on *The House Of Blue Light* were aired to a healthy reception, and as the gathering of hacks excitedly babbled their opinions into each other's ears amid the roar of 'Bad Attitude', 'The Unwritten Law', and the rest, the band (minus one Ritchie Blackmore, who decided he'd be better off at home in Long Island, New York) wandered around, laughing and joking like the best of friends certain rumours would have you disbelieve. Yes, it's a good album alright — in fact, after a mere two or three plays, I'm tempted to report its superiority to *Perfect Strangers* — but I'll reserve final judgement until I've had a chance to really get my teeth into it. I think. However, I do recommend you make every effort to purchase *The House Of Blue Light* immediately. Rock music of this calibre is rare enough these days."

A local Canadian newspaper considered that whilst *Perfect Strangers* had "restored the band to the chart-topping status it had enjoyed several years earlier", *The House Of Blue Light* was a "showcase that nails down the boys' unique mixture of blues and hard rock", stating that 'Bad Attitude' was "one of the most anthemic songs ever recorded by Deep Purple", and that other tracks of note were 'The Unwritten Law' and 'Call Of The Wild'. They surmised that the album was "a batch of killer cuts that jump out at you" with "classic rock with its routes in the seventies and its spirit in the eighties".

Several contributed their opinion on the album to *The Hard Report*: "We expect a few new moves the next time around, but for now, *Blue Light* is a safe and solid step forward on the upper tier of the comeback trail." And "If the initial Deep Purple release of '87 is any indication, this year will be rock and roll heaven." Also; "Deep Purple is back to blow it out for you. Once again, Purp shows all the pretenders what power rock is all about."

From *The Sault Star* (based in Ontario, Canada): "Everyone was rocking at *The House Of Blue Light*. Despite the hype, when Deep Purple reunited in 1984, no one expected any more from it than they did from any of the other bands that had been resurfacing in hopes of gaining a spot at centre stage. But after the release of *Perfect Strangers*, opinions changed. With the original line-up of Ritchie Blackmore, Ian Gillan, Roger Glover, Jon Lord and Ian Paice, Deep Purple sounds even better and more vital than it did on *Perfect Strangers*. The chemistry of the five members seems to have picked up where the band left off in the early seventies when it released classic rock albums like *Fireball* and *Machine Head*. Only now, the originators of heavy metal have refined their music to reach both the hard rockers and the followers of top forty rock. 'Bad Attitude' is the first single and stands a good chance of becoming Deep Purple's first hit in some time. Along with 'Bad Attitude', standout tracks include 'The Unwritten Law', 'Mitzi Dupree' and 'Hard Lovin' Woman'."

From *Rolling Stone*: "Of the seventies hard-rock dinosaurs that still roam the earth, Deep Purple is one of the few with any credibility left in its crunch. *The House Of Blue Light* — the second album by Purple's classic *In Rock* line-up since their return to active duty — is certainly a marked improvement over their lukewarm '84 comeback, *Perfect Strangers,* and, except for a couple of outright duds on side two, is as good as this band has ever been since its 'Smoke On The Water' salad days. 'Bad Attitude' opens the album with five minutes of vintage *Machine Head* sludge — Ian Paice's thunder sticks calling the proceedings to order with a rigid goose-step beat, Ian Gillan raping his tonsils with the vigour of yesteryear. And 'Mad Dog' is basically an '87-model 'Highway Star'; high-speed metal fortified with Jon Lord's lusty Hammond organ sound and the brass-knuckle guitar of Ritchie Blackmore."

"The band has spiked its old hammer-and-anvil sound with a little future tech here and there: 'The Unwritten Law' features subtly deployed electro-hand-claps and percolating sequencer amid its clenched-fist chorus and Blackmore's loco fretwork. But it's only when Purple turns on the retro-charm full blast that *The House Of Blue Light* really goes up in flames. 'Hard Lovin' Woman' and 'Dead Or Alive' are both body-slam rockers in the old blitzkrieg spirit of 'Speed King' and 'Fireball', while Paice's sledgehammer-of-the-gods drumming and Blackmore's punch-your-lights-out chords keep 'Call Of The Wild', with its atypically poppy hook, from turning into neo-Boston fluff."

"Fortunately, all that crash 'n' burn also obscures most of

the album's lyric embarrassments. Although Gillan is hardly the Alan Alda of heavy metal, 'Mitzi Dupree', a heavy-plodding blues, may be a new low in rock-star sexism ('I said what is this queen of the ping-pong business... I said ooh, have another drink...'). But aside from the rather purple poetry, the ho-hum Armageddon stomp 'Strangeways', and a notable lack throughout the album of classic Blackmore psycho-chicken-scratch soloing, *The House Of Blue Light* is a surprisingly strong return from the tar pits. There's no 'Smoke On The Water' here, but Deep Purple still has a pretty good fire going down below."

From *The Ottawa Citizen*: "Anyone who has lost faith in the ability of old dinosaurs to come back from the dead need only look at Deep Purple. After ten years apart, the key line-up reunited, then put out *Perfect Strangers*, which went platinum. The response surprised even the band itself. This does not only comment on Deep Purple's talents, it says something about the current generation of rock fans. They do not automatically see older bands as has-beens, but more often musicians with a legend behind them. Deep Purple draws on that legendary sound, but does not use it as a crutch. With this release, the band takes yet a more freewheeling approach to its music than it did with *Perfect Strangers*. One might have thought Deep Purple would be tempted to follow up the success of *Perfect Strangers* with more of the same. But *The House Of Blue Light*, which takes its title from a line in the Deep Purple classic, 'Speed King', takes a courageous creative step. It includes progressive rock elements without diminishing the hard drive of the music."

"In the seventies, Deep Purple did much to create a framework for hard rock. Here, they embellish it while at the same time recouping that raw enthusiasm for power rock it had when the band started out many years ago. The brand of metal music that the band helped pioneer has no parameters, which is what makes this endeavour all commendable. Deep Purple has not only managed to come back and keep stride, it is pacing one step ahead of the pack, which is no small accomplishment. *The House Of Blue Light* is a consistent, solid set of music that has what it takes to be one of the key hard rock albums of this decade."

The Tyne and Wear newspaper, the *Gateshead Post* candidly said; "*The House Of Blue Light* — the return of the bane of my life! When I was a snotty second former at comprehensive school, all my friends talked about was rock music, and Deep Purple were top of the pile. Their name was everywhere, scrawled on sports bags in mock Gothic style, etched on the walls of toilets, and proudly displayed on condensation-covered windows. The strange thing was this was early 1977, and the band had split up over a year before. Yet they still held a magnetic fascination to rock fans young and old. Punk came and went, and so did several other musical styles and fads, but Purple always had their faithful following."

"Peter still talked of Ritchie Blackmore, Ian Gillan and the rest with hushed reverence, being careful not to blacken the name. Compilations of greatest hits arrived, topped the charts, then disappeared as suddenly as they had arrived, and then, in early 1984, the rumours, always around, started again stronger than ever — Deep Purple were to reform! Well they did, and no one really took any notice apart from the old faithful, some of whom compared the *Perfect Strangers* LP to the old band's finest moments and decided quite rightly that Ritchie and company should not have bothered."

"That LP and *The House Of Blue Light* are the work of a different band, the same members maybe, but so many years on that they should not be compared to the old Purple. I wasn't a fan of them, but it is clear that stuff like 'Smoke On The Water', 'Black Night', 'Child In Time' and all the other anthems were a cut or two above most other rock music of the time. The songs on *The House Of Blue Light* however, are just plain bad. From the opening 'Bad Attitude' to the closing 'Dead Or Alive', this LP is devoid of new ideas and real energy. For solace, I turned to the lyric sheet, always a source of a good laugh. There are several classic lines on this record, but the most hilarious has to be 'She walked into the room/Her hand upon her hip/Said look out boy'll make your backbone slip'. I mean, are they serious?"

From *The Columbia Record*: "*Perfect Strangers* was a resounding success, capturing all the fire and spirit of the early days without sounding forced or nostalgic. Fans celebrated Deep Purple's comeback and anxiously awaited the follow-up to *Perfect Strangers*. Well, the new album is here, but I'm afraid it's the kind of record that turns comebacks into tailspins. It's called *The House Of Blue Light*, but "The House Of Being Trite" would be more appropriate. The album fails to maintain Deep Purple's identity as rock and roll innovators. The band members display the same masterful talents and ability that once made them the biggest name in the business, but the problem here is with the songs. They don't deserve the attention of these fine musicians."

"Things get off to a powerful start with 'Bad Attitude', a sneering rocker that displays Gillan in good voice, Paice pounding some thunderous drums, and Blackmore asserting himself with a synthesiser-assisted guitar solo. Things sound pretty good at this point. But somewhere along the line, Deep Purple decided they should be more modern, use the new technology and all that. As a result, songs like 'The Unwritten Law', 'Call Of The Wild', 'Black & White' and 'Dead Or Alive' rely on layers of electronic keyboards instead of Blackmore's searing guitar or Lord's dramatic Hammond organ. 'Mad Dog' has some chunky rhythm guitar chords, and during his solo, Blackmore proves he's still a master of blues-rock phrasing. 'Strangeways' is a cleverly devised song, with enough unexpected changes and intermingling parts to hold your interest. It also packs the most relevance: 'Have you seen the headlines, princess engaged. Three-million out of work, but that's on the second page'."

"The high point of the album is 'Mitzi Dupree', an honest-to-goodness blues rocker. The band throws off the shackles of modern hard rock conventions and returns to their roots of true British heavy metal blues. Blackmore's Stratocaster and Lord's Hammond B-3 soar to familiar heights. Deep Purple should do an entire album of this stuff. Maybe the band was under pressure from the record company to get out another album. Maybe they thought the enthusiasm of their fans would die if they didn't release more "product". But if the fans could wait eleven years for *Perfect Strangers*, they could have surely held out a little longer for a better successor. Whatever the case, if there's to be a third album by the regrouped Deep Purple, let's hope it's done in the same "we've got something to prove" spirit of *Perfect Strangers*."

From New Jersey's *Asbury Park Press*: "*The House Of Blue Light* sounds like one more fine product from a steady-rolling band that's been around and will continue to be around. Not a swan song, not a comeback, not a Best Of, not a solo, not a spin-off, but just a wonderful couple of sides from a band that plays so well together."

"First, the bad news: *Perfect Strangers* this album ain't. Purple's 1984 reunion album just had a quality to it that could only result from an overdue collaboration finally reaching fruition. The general consensus in the rock press was the album reached "all-time" status, right up there with *Zep I*, *Zep II*, *Sgt Pepper's*, *The White Album*, and *Exile On Main St*. One more note on the downside: This is not a Jon Lord album. Neither was *Perfect Strangers*, really. This is a strange development in the Deep Purple story. The band was always famous for having the focus bounce back and forth between Lord's and Blackmore's soloing. Blackmore is as brilliant as he always was, but Lord doesn't step out with a good solid blast of the Hammonds like he used to. But there's plenty to recommend. Standout cuts include 'Hard Lovin' Woman', which is stormy and driving. 'The Spanish Archer' opens like classic Purple: a chord from Lord, with flittering Blackmore licks to kick it off. This one really benefits from Gillan's ever-cynical lyrics. 'Strangeways' gets off on the wrong foot with one of those aforementioned modern gimmicks, but once the song gets cookin', it's vintage Purple. It has a very exotic hook, a kind of spacey musical theme reminiscent of the title track from *Perfect Strangers*."

"A big winner is 'Mitzi Dupree', which you'd have to call Ian Gillan's showcase. Gillan is renowned for his screams. Honest. He sang the part of Jesus on the original *Jesus Christ Superstar* album, and if you want to hear some beautiful screaming, put on side two when he throws those merchants out of the temple. And of course, 'Child In Time', an early Purple classic, is the ultimate song for Gillan screams. Well, 'Mitzi Dupree' has got 'em, folks. And a very nice little story about Gillan's dalliance with a courtesan. It's a smoky, rainy kind of song, the kind a rock star might compose during a reflective period, and Lord throws in a little smoky, rainy piano to help colour that mood. Good stuff!"

"The only bummer of a cut — and maybe it'll get better with time — is 'Call Of The Wild', which is a good song but has a real lame chorus that's obviously aimed at the mainstream. Come on, fellas! All that talk about integrity, and you go and temper your material! Next you'll be hiring Phil Collins to produce you. But it's just a trifle, folks. This is solid work. These guys still have the magic. They're helping to keep hard rock alive, which ain't easy in these days of TV evangelists and styling mousse. Jon Lord's trademark moustache may have turned white since the last album, but him and the boys will always be ready to kick out the jams. Purple, man. It's *deep*."

Is *Perfect Strangers* comparable to *Sgt Pepper's*? In terms of the former's cultural, technological and commercial impact, it could be argued that it didn't quite touch the same kind of heights that The Beatles' iconic album did. Still though, it is noteworthy that *Perfect Strangers* was evidently adored and respected by some to that extent. This very much touches on the idea that what Deep Purple Mk2.2 meant to people on a wider scale, is not necessarily in parallel to what their music meant to fans with a more intense interest in the band.

From Texas' *The Corpus Christi Caller*: "The fickle tides of the pop business strike again. Look at British heavy rockers Deep Purple. When they reunited in 1984, they became a hot commodity in the United States. They sold a million copies of their *Perfect Strangers* album here, even though it barely entered the top twenty on some overseas charts. So what happens with their recent follow-up, *The House Of Blue Light*? It climbs the European charts and goes to number one in Germany, and languishes on the US charts… Part of the trouble has been timing. Deep Purple's album is out at the same time as Bon Jovi and Cinderella, two other Polygram hard rock acts who have received the lion's share of attention. Another drawback may be Deep Purple's refusal to tailor their sound for commercial rock stations… Deep Purple's new album contains plenty of grind-it-out hard rock, again showcasing Gillan's rugged vocals, guitarist Ritchie Blackmore's sonic slashes, and the professional steadiness of the rest of the group. The album may lack the consistency of *Perfect Strangers*, but it again whets the appetite for the band in concert."

With regards to the pressure to make music with increased commercial potential, Gillan said; "We did that once and it was a dismal failure. It was years ago on a song called 'Never Before'. We decided to put every hook in there and went for the funkiest rhythm and most accessible lyrics. Today I look back and call the song 'Never Again'."

The track listing on *The House Of Blue Light* was not the result of a band in agreement. 'Mitzi Dupree' nearly didn't make it. Gillan was happy with it, but Blackmore didn't want it to go on the album — so much so that that which appears on it is from a demo (with the guitarist having refused to do another take).

In all fairness, 'Mitzi Dupree' is very much a Gillan song. He said of his inspiration for it; "I was on a plane going to Salt Lake City when I was in Black Sabbath, and I saw this absolutely amazing boiler. Oh, a sensational lump! So I went over to talk to her, and she said, 'Hi, I'm Mitzi, Mitzi Dupree', and I thought, 'Wow, what a great name!'. I was in love. Anyway, it turned out she was going way up north to a mining town in Canada to do a show. So I asked her what she did, and she told me that she did an act with ping-pong balls. Now, I've actually seen women do this before, in a small room behind a kitchen in Bangkok, and it's absolutely amazing. There was this Siamese girl on stage and there were five Italians in the front row, all with a glass of wine each. She bent over backwards and — pop-pop-pop-pop-pop — these five ping-pong balls were fired out of nowhere and each one landed in a glass — I swear to you! This bird also pulled out fifty double-edged razor blades from the same place, all attached to a bit of cotton. She signed autographs, she did paintings. It was unbelievable! And this was what Mitzi did. 'Mitzi Dupree' is a dead live song. It came out of a jam and we just recorded it for reference. I played it afterwards and thought it was great. I couldn't stop singing it. So I said to Roger, 'We've got to do something with it'. And he said, 'Well, we can write on it, but we don't have to play it again because everyone else hates it'. So we wrote the lyrics and I sang it to the jam tape, and Roger and I decided to leave it like that, because it sounded so natural and spontaneous. It's a great track."

When speaking to a journalist prior to the album's release, Gillan referred to 'Dead Or Alive' as "a pile of shit", adding, "It's just not very good... It's going to be good on stage. Maybe that's why it's on there. I did write it, but under protest, I might add. I think everyone else likes it, but I don't".

Having been put on the backburner during the recording sessions for *Perfect Strangers*, 'The Unwritten Law' was rearranged to include synthesisers, thus making it an incredibly different track compared to what had been done with it back in 1984. "I nearly killed Ritchie when I heard that riff," said Gillan. "It's the most difficult riff I've ever had to write for! I was going around for ages going '*diddle-id, diddle-id*' behind his back."

The fact that everyone in the band seemed less inclined to agree with each other than they had when making *Perfect Strangers* was, by many accounts, a vital catalyst in what came to be the unravelling of the Deep Purple Mk2 reunion. It's worth noting though, that at the time, the press was given a different version of events. Now, whether this was down to a need to tow the line for the benefit of publicity, or whether it was about putting on a brave, professional face, or whether it is only with hindsight that each member of the band realised how bad the situation was, we'll never know.

For instance, this is what Gillan said when doing a promotional interview for *The House Of Blue Light*: "I don't think there's any reason to assume there's a danger of us breaking up again. I want to be in Deep Purple for the rest of my life. And I hope the rest of the band do as well."

Around that time, perhaps he was blissfully unaware of the fact that his days with the band were looking numbered, which would suggest that when they got around to sacking him, the event was all the more painful!

Regardless of what had happened in terms of the teamwork element (or lack thereof) during the making of *The House Of Blue Light*, at the time, Gillan spoke highly of what he considered to be the album's musical merit. "I'm pretty pleased with it," he said, and "It is a good album overall" but "It's going to take another album, I think, for us to get back to as we were in 1970 — in attitudes and everything else... When Purple first got back together, there was a Whitesnake attitude, a Rainbow attitude and a Gillan attitude all mixed up together. But I think the corners will round off gradually, and after the next album, we'll be just right".

Nowadays, the general narrative relating to the making of *The House Of Blue Light* is that it was a difficult and stressful time for all concerned. In retrospective interviews, the album has rarely been spoken of in a positive light by anyone who was involved with it.

Ian Gillan went on to compare the making of *The House Of Blue Light* to the negative experiences he had whilst working on *Who Do We Think We Are*: "Rog and I did a great deal of preparation for what was to become *The House Of Blue Light*, only to find that, by now, Ritchie wasn't interested in listening to any of us... This was going to be a struggle, there was no cohesion, and it reminded me of the time in Rome, years before in 1972, when the circumstances were very similar as we tried to make *Who Do We Think We Are*. Ritchie hated a song called 'Painted Horse', and it was a war trying to get it released at all. Now we had the 'Mitzi Dupree' story, which I worked on with Rog, to give a lyric to one of the rough backing tracks. Ritchie hated it so much, he refused to re-record it, so what you hear on the album is the original demo. It's hard to deal with that sort of thing sometimes, and I didn't. It pissed me off big time. If the chemistry isn't right, if the spirit isn't there, then an album can sound like a struggle. In my humble opinion, *Blue Light* and *Who Do We Think We*

Are fall into that category."

Blackmore told *Burrn*; "The recording of the album took us so long, that even before the release, I was already tired of it. On this album, there wasn't even one successful song. During the recording sessions, the problems already started with Ian Gillan. That's why it took us so much time to finish it. Within the group, we constantly had conflicts, which made it very difficult. So when we finished recording the album, I said: 'I don't want to record another album in such an atmosphere.'... I think some of the songs were good, but I can't think of one that I really liked personally... I'm always interested in making music, but I don't like to spend so much time in the studio, working for days on just one song. I start to lose my interest and enthusiasm. Then I often ask myself: 'What am I doing here?'. I like to play and write music when I feel like it, when I'm in the right mood. On *The House Of Blue Light*, there aren't such songs. Besides, I also don't like the sound of the drums, which is also why I never listened to this record afterwards... I took it as a matter of course. The fact that we have spent so much time on this record, killed all the songs, they didn't sound natural anymore. A really good song is written in something like five minutes. When you listen to these songs, you will realise that some of them are actually not that bad, but the endless editing killed them."

He said to *Guitar* in March 2010; "I think I played like shit on it, and I don't think anyone else really got that into it. To me, it was a bit of a disaster."

Jon Lord told *Modern Keyboard*; "*House Of Blue Light* was a weird album and hard to put together. We made the massive mistake of trying to make our music current. We discovered that people didn't want us to do that."

Lord also said: "This album I found very challenging — more so than *Perfect Strangers*. With *Perfect Strangers* — the album, the tour, and the t-shirt — we had the curiosity factor:

'Are they really back together?', 'Can they do it again?', and so on. We did do it again, and it was highly successful — successful beyond any of our expectations. I mean, in the US, it was the second-highest grossing tour of the year after Bruce Springsteen, which isn't a bad trophy to hang on your wall, is it? The album went platinum in America, and I mean we would have all been knocked out if it had gone gold! So all in all, it was a huge success. But we did have that curiosity factor, and I think that now that curiosity must have died down a little, so we're aware that a lot of the "fringe" people, who came to see us last time just to see what we looked like, might have to be lured this time."

Promotional videos were done for the songs 'Bad Attitude' and 'Call Of The Wild'. Whilst *The House Of Blue Light* sold reasonably well, even Deep Purple themselves didn't have the highest expectations for it.

Such were Gillan and Glover's frustrations with working on *The House Of Blue Light*, that they happily embraced the opportunity to work on an extra-curricular album. It enabled them to get the creative ideas out that they just didn't feel able to do under the band politics of Deep Purple.

Tour manager Colin Hart recalled in his autobiography; "Once the album was finished, Ian and Roger, accompanied by Charlie Lewis and our Canadian engineer Nick Blagona, went off to Montserrat in the Caribbean to do their own album, *Accidentally On Purpose*."

Gillan recalled; "It was not only a release valve after frustrations of the Purple sessions, but also the first time we'd had the chance to work on material unencumbered by the expectations and limitations of a band. We would just write songs. Songs that had their own value. We smoked a little ganja and started to relax. About half of the album was done, but we had to stop as the next Purple tour was about to commence."

The House Of Blue Light-Power: DEEP PURPLE

Very Special Guest: BAD COMPANY

Sie sind halt alte Füchse und so stimmt das Timing zwischen Plattenveröffentlichung und neuer Tournee perfekt. THE HOUSE OF BLUE LIGHT ist der starke LP-Nachzieher zum Comeback-Album PERFEKT STRAN-GERS. – Begrenzt gibt es noch Karten für die Konzerte.

Und daß Ian Gillan, Roger Glover, Jon Lord, Ritchie Blackmore und Ian Paice live zur Sache gehen, als würden sie jungfräulich neu ihr Publikum erobern, hat sich inzwischen rumgesprochen. Mit der Reife und dem gegenseitigen Verstehen wuchs natürlich die Harmonie und kam die ungebrochene Lust wieder, saftigen Rock 'n' Roll zu spielen. Die Purple-Power ist Legende, auf ihrem neuen Album zeigen sie den Jungen, was eine Harke ist. Ausgefeilt, abwechslungsreich die Rocksongs, den zeitgeist treffend und doch bei ihren Worzeln bleibend: „The Spanish Archer" featured Blackmores Gitarrenkünste, monstermäßig leicht orientalisch geht's bei „Strangeways" zu und der Rock-Blues „Mitel Duprée" läßt Purple-Fan-Herzen höher schlagen.

AUF TOUR
DEEP PURPLE
Special Guest:
BAD COMPANY

31. 1. Oldenburg, Weser-Ems-Halle
1. 2. Hannover, Messehalle 7
3. 2. Berlin, Deutschlandhalle
4. 2. Dortmund, Westfalenhalle
6. 2. Saarbrücken, Saarlandhalle
8. 2. Köln, Sporthalle
9. 2. Frankfurt, Festhalle
11. 2. Heidelberg/Eppelheim, Rhein-Neckar-Halle
14. 2. Zürich, Hallenstadion
15. 2. Zürich, Hallenstadion
17. 2. München, Olympiahalle
18. 2. Stuttgart, Schleyerhalle

Living Wreck

By the end of 1986, Deep Purple's tour dates for Europe were being planned with certainty, with the plan not too different to that which the band had followed in 1985. Germany was due to be treated to more performances though, as were places that the band hadn't visited the last time around.

The warm-up gigs in Budapest, Hungary would mark the first time Deep Purple had played behind "the iron curtain" since 1975. When the band and crew got there, they spent three days rehearsing. On the night of the band's second show there, they included a traditional Hungarian tune and Blackmore and Glover swapped guitars for 'Smoke On The Water' as part of the encore.

"I have nothing but confidence about our shows," said Gillan. "The last time, people were coming and thinking, 'Can they still crack it?'. But now they know we can, and they're more relaxed."

In March 1987, one journalist reviewed a live performance for UK paper, *The Observer* (they didn't make it clear which gig they attended, but based on how they discussed how much they enjoyed Purple's performance at Dagenham's Roundhouse in 1970, it is most likely that the following is in reference to a London date): "It was a mixture of curiosity and nostalgia that took me to see the reformed Deep Purple. Nostalgia is a poor taskmaster, but I wanted to see how those years altered my perceptions of their music. The proposition was made all the more intriguing by the line-up being the same much-vaunted Deep Purple Mk2 version that I had seen in

1970. It was a pleasant surprise that Deep Purple, in their way, are still pretty damn good. Their freshness has gone, as has much of Ian Gillan's unique ability to hold penetrating high notes for long periods. There is nothing "progressive" about them now. They play what the audience wants, and most of the songs date back to the seventies."

"It is unusual for a band which split up eleven years ago to remain so popular with the heavy metal audience. But to remain as revered as Deep Purple is truly extraordinary. The reason, I suspect, is that Deep Purple were never really heavy metal. They were, and are, a rock band with their roots in the blues from where they learned the art of writing memorable riff patterns. Ritchie Blackmore learned his licks from the Chicago bluesmen, and underneath the feedback pyrotechnics is a sense of shade and feeling. Jon Lord mainly uses a Hammond B-3 organ, a relic of the 1960s, to produce a heavy Gothic sound like a rabid Bach. In gentler moments he plays Stax soul licks and Jimmy Smith jazz runs."

"A legion of heavy metal musicians have plagiarised Purple licks, removed the subtlety, and produced a largely unrelenting and humourless music. Deep Purple, on the other hand, retain the talent to be varied and interesting while not forgetting they are there to rock. Nothing demonstrates this better than their anthem 'Child In Time' from the *In Rock* album, a slow haunting refrain that builds through twists and turns into a searing guitar solo, and then fades back down again. Deep Purple remain rock's masters of tension and release. 'Dead Or Alive', from their new album *House Of Blue Light* (it does not compare with their early seventies albums), started with a gentle bluesy guitar moving into a hard B.B. King-style blues, through a Santana organ/guitar/congas pattern before unleashing into the song's hard rock format."

"Gillan's audience rabble-rousing and Blackmore's elfish self-parody of rock guitarist acrobatics provides the mainstay of the band's stage presence. Their only weakness is the lyrics, which were never great, but even their new songs are rooted in the limited sexual vocabulary of seventies rock, although AIDS seems to have made an impression. The band returned for two encores. First their 1970 hit single 'Black Night' — in which Gillan ingeniously inserted chunks of the old rock and roll tune, 'Running Bear'. Then they played what the audience had come for: 'Smoke On The Water' — the Deep Purple desert island disc — complete with communal singing and dry ice. The show was a success because, unlike many comebacks, it was neither tacky nor sad, just professional."

The Kansas City Star reported in May 1987; "'We haven't changed at all!' proclaimed Ian Gillan. Why should they? They have at least 10,000 reasons not to. That's how many fans went to Kemper Arena on Tuesday to witness one of the world's last remaining dinosaur hard rock bands. The Deep Purple of Tuesday consisted of the same five members who visited Memorial Hall in 1972. It was an amazing feat in the transitional and youthful world of rock and roll. And Gillan wasn't lying. Although his contemporaries such as Eric Clapton have evolved so much that new hits are virtually at odds with their classics, Deep Purple continues to pound out the same brand of grandiose head splitters, be they new tunes or the warhorses the crowd went to hear."

"Despite modern touches such as laser graphics, the audience probably came as close to a trip back to 1972 as it can get outside of a Led Zeppelin reunion. Highschool fans who are used to the outlandish costumes and tiered stages of today's heavy metal bands were in for a surprise. The band still plays in front of a wall of speakers, with all five members hunkered in close together. The beefy Gillan looked more like a roadie than the star, sporting bushy hair and one of the band's souvenir t-shirts. Keyboardist Jon Lord still drives the group with his patented heavy metal organ sound, even with digital synthesiser technology at his disposal. And the group still plays 'Space Truckin'', not to mention 'Highway Star', the opener, 'Lazy' or 'Woman From Tokyo', all time-honoured crowd pleasers. Deep Purple was never a band to have more than one or two memorable songs from each album, but they were enough to fill out a two-hour show. The classics came in handy because the new album, *The House Of Blue Light*, is one of the group's weakest. The band felt obligated to perform sludge-filled duds such as 'Dead Or Alive' and 'Hard Lovin' Woman'. Strangely, the two winners of the 1985 reunion album, the laser-enhanced 'Perfect Strangers' and 'Knocking At Your Back Door', put the show back on track after the newer setbacks."

"Lord and guitarist Ritchie Blackmore treated the crowd to their classical leanings on solos, and Gillan still proved himself the second-best screamer in rock — next to Robert Plant — even if he did have to leave the stage frequently for something to drink. Admittedly, it's a paradox watching men old enough to be the parents of many audience members pump out rock at gut-crunching levels. Parents who fear heavy metal can rest assured that Gillan was the perfect gentleman host. Perhaps it took age and longevity to give the band the authority its music never did."

The St Louis Post Dispatch reported in May 1987; "In the annals of rock 'n' roll, Deep Purple is certainly a heavyweight. But the members of this legendary heavy metal band resisted the temptation to become bogged down in their own history when they performed at Keele Auditorium Monday night. Instead, they concentrated on material from the two strong albums they've released since they re-formed three years ago. With the addition of a few carefully chosen Deep Purple classics, the concert signalled the reawakening of a sleeping giant."

"The show opened with a spectacular laser display

featuring multicoloured lightning-like flashes across a scenic backdrop. The unmistakable rumblings of Jon Lord's Hammond organ sent shivers up the spine as lead singer Ian Gillan and guitarist Ritchie Blackmore launched into the first of several "duets" which pitted voice against instrument. It was the perfect warm-up for Gillan's high-pitched vocal gymnastics, the kind audiences have come to expect since his *Jesus Christ Superstar* days. With bassist Roger Glover and drummer Ian Paice, this is the Deep Purple line-up that in the late sixties and early seventies covered the gamut from pseudo-classical art-rock to guitar-dominated heavy metal. And so it was Monday night, with Lord's classical/ragtime lead-in to 'Knocking At Your Back Door' and Blackmore's frenzied solo during 'Hard Lovin' Woman'."

"Yet more than any other element, the concert was characterised by a strong ensemble performance that found the group members playing off of each other rather than competing for attention. The phenomenon was most evident during 'Dead Or Alive' when some clever spotlight work highlighted the co-operative effort between Lord and Blackmore. It continued through strong new songs such as 'The Unwritten Law' and 'Perfect Strangers', as well as Deep Purple standards like 'Space Truckin'', 'Woman From Tokyo' and 'Smoke On The Water'."

Gillan said of the setlist around that time; "What do you leave out? We'd get crucified if we left out some of the classics. How much new stuff should we use? How much from *Perfect Strangers*? 'Smoke On The Water' is so strong, so fantastic. It's like a machine we will climb on every night, the same with 'Highway Star'. The only song that's hit or miss for me is 'Child In Time'. The band loves to play it, but the song's mood is so delicate, so elusive, that for me, it's either fantastic or terrible."

Under the heading of "Deep Purple Brings Its Original

Sound Into The Eighties", Ohio's *Akron Beacon Journal* reported in May 1987; "The jackets were fringed, the hair was frizzy and the music was psychedelic. But the year was undoubtedly 1987. When the air at the Coliseum on Monday smacked of the seventies, the music performed was peculiarly current. More than half of the full-house crowd that packed the hall to see Deep Purple couldn't have been alive when the British heavy metal band formed in 1968."

"Guitarist Ritchie Blackmore, who left the band in 1975 to form Rainbow, led the five-member group through self-indulgent jams that had just enough moments of inspiration to keep things interesting. Blackmore and keyboardist Jon Lord performed their obligatory "even though I play this kind of music, I'm still a good musician" interludes that included musical quotes from Joplin, Gershwin and even Beethoven. Ludwig Van's 'Ode To Joy' was even accompanied by the most extravagant laser show of the evening. Vocalist Ian Gillan, bassist Roger Glover and drummer Ian Paice joined Blackmore and Lord in performing everything from oldies such as 'Child In Time' to such newer tunes as 'Perfect Strangers'. Monster movie riffs abounded in the post-reformation Deep Purple numbers, suggesting the reasons for the group's popularity among today's technological-minded teens. But even when playing songs that still waver between the immortal and the dated, like 'Space Truckin'', Deep Purple maintain some integrity. The flamboyant costumes and choreographed staging common to most heavy metal bands of the eighties were conspicuously missing from the band's show. Deep Purple still looked, acted and sounded like Deep Purple. And the kids didn't even know it."

The review in the *Hartford Courant* of the performance that took place at the Hartford Civic Centre was less than flattering: "The sound emanating from the Hartford Civic Centre Friday night was that of dinosaurs rising from the dead of giant anachronisms, lumbering around the stage, giving off ear-shattering wails and crunching music in their wake with their sheer brute strength. It was the sound of Deep Purple, the hard rock group of the late sixties and early seventies that was the precursor of heavy metal. It was a sound that the crowd of nearly 12,000 loved. It was also the sound that bordered on the irresponsible."

"In its heyday, the British band had the distinction of being the loudest rock band, even achieving a notation in the *Guinness Book of World Records*. And although the human ear hasn't changed dramatically in fifteen years, audio technology has. Deep Purple proved that it could play till it hurts — and then some. But there was little critical pleasure in the pain."

"It was a concert filled with rock clichés, indulgent playing, endless solos, corny special effects, and a sense that these performers were playing for our sins. It was rock 'n' roll hell. It didn't start out that way. When the band regrouped three years ago, there was a sense of event, with the founding fathers of heavy metal returning for a piece of the financial pie. And who could blame them? Heavy metal was now big business, and they, after all, helped give it its start. Although their album, *Perfect Strangers*, was a modest success, the arena tour was a surprise smash. The band's second album, *The House Of Blue Light*, didn't make much of an impact this year on the charts. But once again the chance to see Deep Purple live is attracting impressive crowds, mostly teenage males. The band has started this month on its latest world tour."

"The Hartford show got off to a rocky start with some technical glitches, centred mainly on Jon Lord's non-playing keyboards. But even after the problems were straightened out, the show was uncoordinated and ragged. Kinder folks could call it playful and loose. For much of the show, the band focused on recent tunes such as 'Perfect Strangers', 'The

Unwritten Law', 'Knocking At Your Back Door', 'Dead Or Alive', with a few lesser known or older tunes, such as 'Child In Time' and 'Black Night', reluctantly thrown in. The band didn't make it to the big old guns such as 'Smoke On The Water' or 'Space Truckin'' until late in the show."

"Ian Gillan was still solid and tough on the vocals. He even managed to do a bit of *Jesus Christ Superstar*. Roger Glover and Ian Paice were fine on rhythms. But Lord was insufferable on the keyboards. His solo spot offered a mishmash of show-off styles that tapped into classical, boogie-woogie, ragtime and rock, succeeding none too well in any of them. Ritchie Blackmore showed that he is still a vital guitar hero, though as the show progressed, his playing turned to ravings."

A week following the above review, a disgruntled fan wrote to the paper, expressing their annoyance at the harsh criticism the journalist had dished out:

"After immensely enjoying the Deep Purple show at Hartford Civic Centre, I was sorely disappointed by *The Courant*'s review. The only "rock 'n' roll hell" was having to read such an inaccurate piece of journalism, which itself bordered on the irresponsible. I do not concur with your reviewer that older tunes were just "thrown in" and must believe they are only lesser known to him because of his lack of interest in the band. This is most unbecoming for a professional journalist. I was very satisfied with the concert. Deep Purple still has the musical energy I enjoyed so in my younger years. Unlike your reviewer, I was impressed with Jon Lord's attempts at different musical styles during his solo, and thoroughly enjoyed Ritchie Blackmore's "indulgent playing" and "endless solos". This was the sound of Deep Purple, and I'm glad it's back. If it was such a pain for your reviewer, perhaps he is in the wrong business."

During a performance in Phoenix on May 30th 1987, Blackmore injured his finger. He threw his Stratocaster in the air and caught it awkwardly. He managed to finish the show — with difficulty and in pain — but it ultimately resulted in all remaining tour dates being postponed until further notice.

Immediately after the injury, the future of the tour was very much in limbo, with hopes that the band would be able to get back to work sooner than they actually did. The *Fort Worth Star-Telegram* reported on 3rd June 1987; "A finger injury suffered by guitarist Ritchie Blackmore Monday night has forced Deep Purple to postpone its Friday night concert at the Tarrant County Convention Centre. The concert will be rescheduled as soon as possible, according to Pace concerts official Vicki Krone. In addition to the Fort Worth show, concerts have also been postponed in Denver, Oklahoma City, Houston, San Antonio, Little Rock, Nashville and Atlanta. Blackmore suffered the injury during the final number of Deep Purple's concert in Phoenix Monday. 'Deep Purple was playing 'Space Truckin''. Ritchie threw the guitar up, went to catch it, and it landed wrong on his finger,' Krone said. 'We're not sure if it's a break or a sprain, but it's bad enough that they've had to postpone several shows. However, it's not so severe that they're going to cancel the shows. It looks like they'll end up postponing about two weeks' worth of concerts, then reroute the schedule so that they can make up the shows as soon as possible. We'll announce a new Fort Worth date as soon as possible.' More than 7,000 tickets had been sold for the Tarrant County Convention Centre date. 'We were looking for close to a sell-out there,' Krone said. 'All the dates were doing very well'."

Gillan and Glover used the postponement to their advantage. For it was then that they went to Minot Studio in New York and then the Power Station to finish *Accidentally On Purpose*, something that had also given them a break from the stresses of being in Deep Purple whilst on the road.

Gillan asserted; "Although *The House Of Blue Light*

wasn't going to set the world on fire, the tour started well and got better. Rog and I decided to take a bus while the other guys made their own arrangements. This would give us the chance to write some more stuff for *Accidentally On Purpose*, while cruising through the countryside and enjoying the scenery. No rush, no airports, no packing and unpacking, party when you want, sleep it off in your bunk. It's the only way to go."

Accidentally On Purpose was released in February 1988, it also spawned the singles, 'Dislocated' in December 1987 and 'She Took My Breath Away' in January 1988. It was a worthwhile project in the sense that at the time, Gillan was still signed to Virgin Records and was contracted to provide them with more product anyway. Gillan and Glover performed the tracks 'Dislocated' and 'Via Miami' on *Friday Night Live* on 25th March 1988.

In his autobiography, Colin Hart asserted that on the tour to promote *The House Of Blue Light*, there were times where the shows sounded good and where, off stage, Blackmore and Gillan were managing to be civil towards each other. Unfortunately though, things can't have been that good overall, as this is the tour now famous amongst fans for having "that incident with the spaghetti" (or whatever you want to call it). It is unclear as to exactly where/when the event took place. In his autobiography, Gillan said he thought it was somewhere in Britain, whilst in a post on a fan forum online, Cooky Crawford (Blackmore's guitar tech from 1981 to 1988) recalled that it took place in Cleveland, Ohio (as did Colin Hart). Either way, it just goes to show that when things were bad, they were *really bad*.

This is Hart's account of what happened: "Roger just took it all in, glad to be back on the road... Most of the time, dates end up a blur in your consciousness, but Richfield Coliseum, Cleveland on May 11th stood out as a day lifted from the mundane. Ritchie squished a plate of spaghetti into Ian's face on the pretext that the singer had somehow "spiked" it. Cool! Now, Ian is not a small guy, and I fully expected World War III to instantly break out, as did Ritchie, who put up his fists Queensbury Rules style, which on reflection now was hilarious, as Ian would have just kicked him in the bollocks. No, Ian, seriously pissed off, but in wonderful and surprising control, got up imperiously, told the guitarist that fighting was not happening and disappeared into the bathroom to clean up, shutting the door behind him. Ritchie just stood there with all of us just looking at him stony-faced. I half expected someone to say that he should have had the carbonara instead. He went back to his room. The following show, understandably, was not the best they'd done."

From his autobiography, this is Gillan's account: "One of the last memories of that tour is a dressing room incident after one of the British dates. The relationship between Ritchie and I simmered and was strained, and on one occasion it cracked. I was in the room when Ritchie burst in furious, a china dinner plate in his hand. On the plate was spaghetti, which someone had smothered in ketchup — given how things were between us, I guess he assumed it was my doing. He raced over to me and said, 'Did you do this?', but before I could open my mouth, he smashed the plate into my face as if it were a custard pie. I slowly stood up, and he started dancing around me with his fists up, saying, 'Come on, then, come on'. I said, 'I don't want to hit you, Ritchie', and turned and walked into the bathroom, where I cried with such rage and frustration and said, 'I quit'. I changed my mind within seconds as I realised how little it would achieve, and it was downhill all the way from there."

Looking back at the logistics and economics of the tour, even if there were moments where musically, the band were on top form, it was plausibly less successful than the 1985 tour. Sure, the 1985 tour was a hard one to beat by any stretch of the imagination, but all the same, the tour in support of *The House Of Blue Light* had a lot of additional — and exceptional — problems to what any band might be able to expect on any typical tour.

Glover confirmed that a UK tour of smaller venues had been given serious consideration for 1987. Not only were the band in disagreement about how to proceed on this, but even if everyone had been up for it, Gillan's status as a tax exile would have made it impossible anyway.

In 1988, a larger-scale tour of America had been lined up. The plan was to start in Saratoga in the July. Dates for this tour were even included as part of advertisements for the live double LP *Nobody's Perfect*, but by August, the vast majority of them had been cancelled.

Although the official reason given was that the album hadn't been released and needed to be remixed, it was more likely due to poor ticket sales. 1985 had carried with it a sense of "can the band do this?" and "what are they like now?". With that element of wonder no longer in play, it makes sense as to why it may have been harder for promoters to generate the same extent of enthusiasm for Deep Purple that had been there at the beginning of the reunion.

Two festival appearances were cancelled (Springfield and Providence) but the band were still welcomed to Giants Stadium in East Rutherford. Even then though, the headlining spot was given to Aerosmith, who were very much on the up commercially around this time following their 1986 collaboration with Run-D.M.C. on a remake of 'Walk This Way', and their 1987 multi-platinum album, *Permanent Vacation*.

Last-minute cancellations were a continuous theme across 1988 for Deep Purple, with one gig set for Spain on 5th October reportedly cancelled just a day prior.

Considering the number of bootlegs that had surfaced by

the time *Nobody's Perfect* was released in June 1988, it could be considered that the band had missed an opportunity there; many fans had already heard what they sounded like live by that point. "When we reunited in 1984, we always felt we were better live than we are in the studio — more exciting," said Glover. "But we felt we shouldn't do a live album straight away. Now, after two studio albums, the timing's much better."

The album's launch party was done with a medieval theme, instigated by Blackmore. Whilst the band members in attendance dressed up in suitable medieval costumes, Jon Lord chose not to take part and stayed away.

According to *Billboard* in July 1988, *Nobody's Perfect* was sold in the US with a promo sticker announcing it as featuring "the best songs, the best line-up". Although it would be easy to write off *Nobody's Perfect* as a contractual obligation album (Gillan said that it "filled the gap because we weren't ready to do another studio album."), it would seem unfair to say that no efforts were made to give it a fighting chance.

"We always felt that if we did another live album, it would have to be honest," said Glover. "So this is honest; *Nobody's Perfect* is us — warts and all."

The album spawned a single, 'Hush'. It had live versions of 'Dead Or Alive' and 'Bad Attitude' on the B-side. In celebration of the band's roots, 'Hush' had been recorded in February 1988 as part of a jam session. Blackmore said that they also had a go at doing 'Black Night', but that it did not turn out very well. Although a video was made to promote 'Hush', the band only appear in it as part of some older footage filmed at their 1985 gig in Providence.

With regards to the recording of 'Hush', Glover said at the time; "We thought of doing it in the live act but never got around to it. It was Ian Gillan's suggestion. It's an honest studio jam. There are a few overdubs, but not many. Ninety percent of the vocals were live with a solo and harmonica added. It came out to be a bit of fun, an irreverent approach. To try and improve on 1968, it could never be; that's the way the band was then."

Despite the fact that *Nobody's Perfect* was met with much criticism when it came out, and that even today, it abundantly divides opinion amongst many Deep Purple fans, it's important to consider that at the time, a lot of thought had gone into the production side of things, especially when it came to Roger Glover's input. Speaking to a journalist around the time of the album's release, he said, "It was a hard task, but a labour of love".

Glover explained how the band had recorded every show on its 1987 tour for the purpose of capturing spontaneous performances, and to avoid wooden results; "We thought it was a good idea to have a twenty-four-track on the road, since there are often times when you come off stage and have had a great night that you think, 'Wouldn't it have been great to have recorded that?'."

After the tour, Glover was tasked with the job of going through hundreds of hours of tape. The German dates weren't an option though ("We didn't play very well there," he said). Once he had selected the strongest options, he got the whole band together to choose five, six or seven versions of any particular song, after which he then selected the winning takes. Not that there was a shortage of material anyway, but if not for Blackmore's finger injury, Glover would have had even more recordings to choose from!

In fact, the only thing that prevented *Nobody's Perfect* from potentially being a triple-LP was the band's acknowledgement that it would be "a lot to listen to". Deep Purple also asked if *Nobody's Perfect* could be released as a double-CD version, with the record company considering that the price of such product would be too expensive for the average fan. The CD therefore offered, according to Glover, "a shorter version of everything". Also, 'Bad Attitude' was released only on the LP and cassette versions of the album, whilst 'Dead Or Alive' only made it onto the cassette release.

In terms of how *The House Of Blue Light* hadn't taken off in America to the extent that had been hoped for, by mid-1987, Glover said that their latest release "has no real rawness there, which is the way Deep Purple sounds best... The essence of Deep Purple is live, in concert. Studio albums are kind of a necessary compromise." It is thus plausible that he saw *Nobody's Perfect* as an opportunity to succeed where the latter studio album hadn't.

From Oregon's *Statesman Journal*: "It seems to me that four sides of music is far too long to sit through just to get to 'Hush' and 'Smoke On The Water'. Besides, who needs two live LPs from a dead act? They can stage all the reunions they want, their best days are far behind them."

From *The Gazette* (in Montreal, Canada): "A four-sided live album with only twelve songs on it? It must be Deep Purple. Seems to me that live versions of most of these songs have already been released. This is truly unnecessary, but not as unnecessary as the band's next studio album, the prospect of which hangs over our collective heads like a musical sword of Damocles."

Canada's *Nanaimo Daily News* said *Nobody's Perfect* was "recorded live during the boys' sold-out 1987 *House Of Blue Light* tour. Their performances throughout that tour were heralded as their best ever, as this double album demonstrates. Worth checking out here: 'Hush' (the band's first hit), 'Strange Kind Of Woman' (featuring an excerpt from the title song of the *Jesus Christ Superstar* musical), 'Smoke On The Water' (a number four Billboard hit single), as well as several other Purple classics: 'Bad Attitude', 'Highway Star', 'Woman From Tokyo', etc. All in all, this new live recording serves as a perfect reminder of Deep Purple's live prowess."

From *The Boston Globe*: "Deep Purple set the standard for keyboard-blasted power rock with a live double album *Made In Japan*. Like *Made In Japan*, the set begins with 'Highway Star', but from there, it's low compression in the travel lane — staid professionalism from the mature band that sounds old. 'Space Truckin'' gets jack-knifed, 'Smoke On The Water' fizzles, 'Child In Time' is bad opera. The title of 'Lazy' sums up the work. When vocalist Ian Gillan shouts 'I can't hear you' during one particularly lame intro, it's hard to tell if he's addressing the audience or the band. Gillan's impromptu version of Buddy Holly's 'Every Day', and phoney yelping to *Jesus Christ Superstar* borders on the ridiculous, as does a studio jam of the band's sixties relic, 'Hush'. And this stuff isn't even recorded that well. Wait for the CD version of *Made In Japan*. *Nobody's Perfect* is no substitute."

From Pennsylvania's *The Morning Call*: "Oh, the temptation to make good use of this album title! Deep Purple's newest is a double live disc (sound familiar?) that shows the band is stuck firmly in the days when it was so outrageous it could legitimately name an album "Who Do We Think We Are". *Nobody's Perfect* comes up far short of the level Purple set with its *Made In Japan* double live disc of fifteen years ago. In fact, you can find almost all of the *Made In Japan* songs here, with a few "newer" tunes thrown in, including a studio remake of their 1968 hit, 'Hush'. Guitarist Ritchie Blackmore is all over the place as usual, Ian Gillan shows he's lost more than a step after screaming for fifteen-plus years, and Jon Lord does the same classical power chord keyboard bit that he's done forever. Perfectly redundant."

From *The Hard Report*: "Over the years, few bands have endured the horrors of the road quite so well or as often as this one. Well into their second decade, their new double live set not only provides us with an excellent example of live musicianship, but also serves to document the band's history... All of the tracks are reminders of the influence and popularity that these guys have been privy to over the years. There are very few surprises to be found here. Everything you could want to hear has been included, as well as the ten-minute epic 'Child In Time', and a jammed-out eleven-minute version of 'Knocking At Your Back Door'... The band members themselves seem to possess a youth and vitality that one can only hope to have at their age, not to mention their performances of 'Highway Star', 'Woman From Tokyo' and 'Black Night' only exemplify that. Also, check out 'Strange Kind Of Woman', 'Lazy' and 'Hush'."

Whilst *Nobody's Perfect* was being mixed at Oxfordshire's Hook End Manor in early 1988, it had already been decided that Deep Purple would spend over a year working on the next studio album, with a release date of January 1990 having been pencilled in. Not much had been done towards it by that point though. As Gillan said shortly after, "I hadn't written one note or one word. All I'd heard was ideas, really."

Not that the singer was necessarily failing to pull his weight though! He explained; "That was the way we'd always worked. There was no point in doing anything until Ritchie was happy with his riff because it was just as likely to be changed anyway. There was no point going in with fresh ideas — that's how the Gillan/Glover album *Accidentally On Purpose* came about. I'd spent ages with Roger prior to recording *The House Of Blue Light*. We had a book full of material — a *ton* of material, which we took up to New England or somewhere, and within a day we'd thrown the book out the window, there just wasn't any point. Ritchie only wanted to do what he wanted to do, and wouldn't really entertain any other ideas. It was as simple as that. But fair enough, it had always worked in the past. I thought it was a shame that people with the talent of Jon Lord and Roger seemed to be closed out. Maybe they're not now, maybe they won't be. But it was difficult."

"In November '88 I was invited *not* to attend a writing session because Ian Paice and Jon Lord wanted to. There'd been all these discussions about writing — a few complaints that it was a closed shop between Roger and myself as far as lyrics and tunes were concerned, which of course is not true. The only reason we did it is because we *did* it! We'd been a songwriting team for many years, but if Paicey or Jon had come up with some words or tunes, I'd have been happy to sing them. Although I've not *heard* any, and they've never shoved any bits of paper under my nose!"

Glover said of his songwriting rapport with Gillan; "See the way we work — Ian and I — we get our space. And that space could be anywhere. Wherever it is we find it. If we're in the studio, maybe there's a certain corner in the control room where we'll put our books and pencils and erasers and rulers and pads. Drinks. Our little area. And what we'll do then is, we'll have a few beers and we'll sit down and just talk about anything. We're good friends. We talk about things in the past or things that have happened to us. Things we read in the newspaper or things that annoyed us. Stories of girls. Whatever. And out of that comes the songs, usually based on some grain of truth."

Following Deep Purple's 1988 dates in Germany, they spent the time in the run-up to Christmas writing and rehearsing in Stowe, Vermont. Ian Gillan was dismissed from the sessions, which saw him returning home to the UK.

By January 1989, the band were sending the singer tapes of what they'd done so far in order that he could get to work on writing the lyrics. The plan was for all of the writing to be done and ready in preparation for the band's return to the studio, which had already been booked for April.

January 1989 was also a vital month for Deep Purple in terms of how they left Polygram Records and signed to BMG.

An April of recording for their new label wasn't to be

though. "I remember when I first heard the news that I had been sacked, from my manager Phil Banfield," said Gillan. "I was in my home studio. I put the phone down, looking pretty pale and shocked, and my wife came in — which she never normally does, because it's like my private hideaway. She said, 'What's the matter with you?'. And I said, 'The bastards just fired me!'."

"I can't imagine why it's happened," he said. "I just can't figure it. Other than what I've said — or the fact that I banged my fist on the table a couple of times and shouted. Jon Lord once said, 'You've gone too far this time, Ian. You've gone too far!'. All I'd said was, 'Why don't we fucking get off our asses and do something?!'. I got fired up and had probably had a couple of drinks too many. I'd knocked the old boys' network. It was not the gentlemanly thing to do, I imagine. I just don't know. I get the feeling that I'd just been sort-of tolerated. They all thought I was slightly mad or something. I didn't fit in with the rest of the guys socially at all — that slightly jet-setter type of life."

As the months rolled on, they were still without a singer. By August 1989, *Music & Media* described the situation as follows: "Deep Purple have put out a statement about Ian Gillan's departure from the band. 'The reason is entirely and categorically due to "musical differences"', say the remainder of Purple, who are looking for a replacement vocalist to start recording the album, due for new year release. However, Gillan begs to differ. 'References by Deep Purple to "musical differences" are just hogwash,' he says in his own statement. 'I thought my days might be numbered when I publicly referred to the manager as a "dickhead" last year and repeated the statement at a full band meeting a few months ago.' He says he has severed all ties with Purple except for Roger Glover, with whom he may record again in the future. In the meantime, Gillan has written eight songs for a solo album in collaboration with the Australian producer Jimbo Barton and is currently shopping around for a record deal."

Jon Lord told *Metal Hammer*; "I think Ian slipped out of position during the last three months and went in an opposite direction. He never seemed to agree to a decision that we made. At last we came to the opinion — and not just Ritchie, don't believe that — that it was not worth it to carry on with him. The enjoyment factor in this band was so high — it's what I was doing the major part of my musical life, with one holiday in Whitesnake — that we didn't want to let the band go down this way... He wasn't giving us anything back. I don't want to criticise Ian as an artist. He is marvellous and I love him."

When asked why things were done "so coldly", Lord said; "I suppose a sense of embarrassment would be the best answer to that. We felt happier that our manager should do it. You'd call it almost cowardly, I suppose, if you wanted to be perfectly honest. It was only that we thought it would be cleaner... We felt that he [Gillan] was distancing himself more and more from the band. He had his own management, he refused to be managed by our manager. He was openly scathing about our manager. Contrary to what he believes, he was not sacked because he didn't like our manager. That's bullshit. We decided he should terminate his employment with us because we didn't think he was pulling in the same direction. It's a sad fact, but true."

Roger Glover said, "It was a very painful period leading up to the decision. I called him [Gillan] up afterwards to say we were still friends. The last Purple album we made, *The House Of Blue Light*, had been a very difficult one to make, not a happy one. The band didn't record it the way I wanted. I'm not the leader, but I am the producer, and I had very strong ideas about the way we should have made the album, and the band didn't want to do it that way. It turned out to be a stiff of an album, and with a very wooden feel about it."

"Roger is the first person I spoke to. A couple of months went by before that happened," said Gillan. "It was quite a blow to the ego. I was Purple's greatest advocate. And to this day, no matter what's gone down, I've still got fond memories of all the boys. I can't turn around and say he's a bastard. They have their moments. It's difficult. I spoke to Roger and his first words were 'I don't know what to say, mate. I'm sorry, it was beyond my control'. And I said, 'Of course I know you had nothing to do with it. You don't even have to say that'. I know where the power base lies in the Purple camp."

Following this comment, Gillan didn't elaborate on his hint about who held the power. Based on what is known now, it would be easy to assume that he was referring to Blackmore, but essentially, that may not have been the case. For indeed, as was proven to be apparent later down the line, *nobody's* position in Deep Purple was truly safe.

It would be unfair to say that Gillan's time away from Deep Purple prior to his re-joining in August 1992 wasn't fruitful. He had formed his own bands before and was willing and able to do so again. The result this time around was Garth Rockett And The Moonshiners. A band to support Gillan as a solo artist, the initial line-up was Mark Buckle on keyboards, Keith Mulholland on bass, Louis Rosenthal on drums, and, on guitars, Harry Shaw and Steve Morris. Having been frustrated with Purple's lack of touring activity, Gillan started a tour with Garth Rockett And The Moonshiners in February 1989.

Gillan's first solo album, *Naked Thunder*, was released in July 1990. It spawned a number of singles — 'Nothing But The Best', 'No More Cane On The Brazos' and 'No Good Luck' — all of which failed to chart, despite their musical merit. Notably though, the album got to number sixty-three in the UK and to number twenty-seven in Sweden. Although it was a far cry from the singer's achievements with Deep Purple, it wasn't an outright flop by any means. In fact, *Naked*

Thunder was promoted as a debut Ian Gillan solo album; his previous releases under the Ian Gillan Band and Gillan names had specifically been group albums.

Although the singer later went on to express dissatisfaction with the album, calling it "rather hum-de-dum", the fact is that at the time, he was keen to stay creative, and keen to keep working. Even though things weren't going tremendously well for him commercially during this period, a sacking from a legendary band could not take that away from him.

May 1989 marked the start of a thirteen-date UK tour for Garth Rockett And The Moonshiners. By the July though, the band was put on the backburner following a charity gig.

By 1990, Gillan was back on the road — with a line-up of Steve Morris, Tommy Eyre (keyboards), Dave Lloyd (backing vocals), Mick O'Donoghue (guitar) and the Sensational Alex Harvey Band's rhythm section of Ted McKenna (drums) and Chris Glenn (bass).

Simply billed as a solo artist to promote *Naked Thunder*, they toured regularly — more so than Deep Purple, in fact! The packed tour schedule was everything that Gillan had been pushing for prior to his departure from Deep Purple, which had been much to the disagreement of some of his band mates.

Also whilst out of Deep Purple, Gillan participated in a re-recording of 'Smoke On The Water' with Rock Aid Armenia. A charity record to raise funds for the victims of an earthquake, the track featured Gillan with Bryan Adams, Tony Iommi, David Gilmour, Roger Taylor, Brian May, Bruce Dickinson and Paul Rodgers. Ironically perhaps, Blackmore also played on the record, although paths were not crossed between him and Gillan; the guitarist only made his contribution once the studio was empty of the other stars.

A second solo album, *Toolbox*, was released in October 1991 — originally just in Europe, Japan and Brazil on the German label EastWest. It was Gillan's last solo album prior to his return to Deep Purple in August 1992. Despite the album's lack of commercial success, the ten-month tour in support of it proved Gillan to be a strong live attraction in certain territories that were generally starved of rock music. The band even played the Faroe Islands! Shows closer to home didn't fare as well though, with one poorly-advertised gig in Milton Keynes attracting only a small audience.

Although Gillan's solo band went through some line-up changes, by the end of its tenure, they had toured Europe, the US and Russia — not bad considering that, in speaking candidly, the singer was clearly hurt that Deep Purple had booted him out.

Rumours of Deep Purple reunions had been doing the rounds since around 1978. Eventually it was announced to the press in April 1984 that the classic Mk2 line-up had reformed. (Pictorial Press Ltd / Alamy Stock Photo)

22nd May 1985. The rather unassuming building is Horizons, where *Perfect Strangers* was recorded. The first new album by Mk2 in twelve years.
Left to right: Crew member Charlie Lewis, Ian Gillan, Raymond D'Addario (production manager), Ian Paice and Jon Lord. (Colin Hart)

Putting the finishing touches to *Perfect Strangers*. Paice and Glover with engineer Nick Blagona. (Colin Hart)

The first reunion gig of sorts. During the mixing of *Perfect Strangers* in Hamburg, the band did an impromptu set in a club. With no keyboards available to play, Jon Lord watched from the bar. (Mick Gregory)

After recording the album, rehearsals began for the imminent world tour. The band chose St Peter's Hall in Bedford. (Bedford Journal)

The band was soon racking up gold discs for sales of *Perfect Strangers*. (Tony Mottram)

Following the release of *Perfect Strangers*, the world tour kicked off in Australia in November '84. It was a huge success and went through to August '85. Perhaps surprisingly though, Deep Purple only played one show in their homeland — at Knebworth — on the wettest June day on record. (Alan Perry Concert Photography)

When it came to writing material for the reunion, Ritchie Blackmore contributed an abundance of ideas. Some tracks — including 'Wasted Sunsets' and 'Perfect Strangers' — were ideas he had been toying with since the Rainbow days of *Difficult To Cure*.
(Alan Perry Concert Photography)

All shots taken backstage after the gig at Limburghal, Genk, Belgium, 24th June 1985.
(Marc Brans)

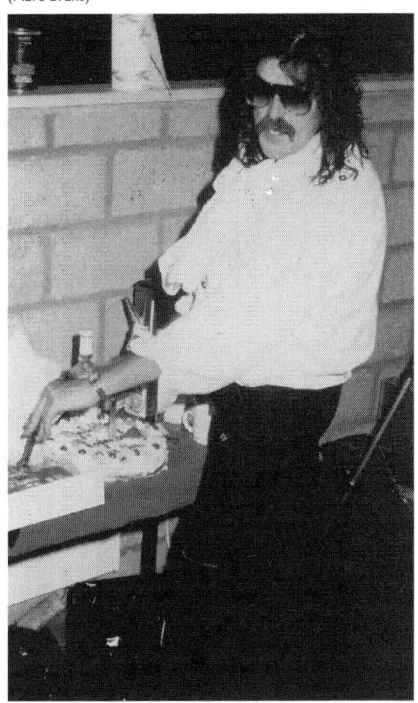

Gillan, Paice and Glover, all looking rather bored at a press conference in Cologne, 8th February 1987. (Marc Brans)

Wembley Arena, March 1987. During the 1987 tour, the band was still performing well, but the petty wranglings between Blackmore and Gillan started to unfold. Also, the resulting live album was seen as a disappointment by Polygram, and before long, Purple switched labels. (Bob Blackham)

16th September 1988. A travel day in Italy. The two hours on stage every night were offset with countless hours of everything else… including sleeping. (Colin Hart)

5th December 1989. Arguably Deep Purple's lynchpin, Roger Glover was always the one who burnt the midnight oil, slaving away in the studio long after the others had done their work.
(Colin Hart)

After one album and tour with Joe Lynn Turner, Mk2 returned with *The Battle Rages On...* and what turned out be a rather brief tour. Although the fans welcomed Ian Gillan back, the feuds with Blackmore continued. Only this time it was the guitarist who became more isolated as the tour rolled on. At Birmingham where these photos were taken, his actions are still talked about to this day. His departure after the show in Helsinki on 17th November 1993 saw the end of Purple's classic line-up for the final time. (Rob Reynolds)

The Battle Rages On...

With Gillan out of the band, Joe Lynn Turner was brought in on vocals. The result was the 1990 album, *Slaves And Masters*. It was met with a mixed reception from fans, many of whom were annoyed that a) the line-up was no longer Mk2 in its entirety, and b) the group was two-thirds Rainbow.

At the time, Gillan asserted that the group responsible for the *Slaves And Masters* album would have been better off calling themselves something other than Deep Purple.

When asked for his thoughts on his successor, Gillan said; "I don't know how Joe Lynn Turner is gonna sound, even if they do anything other than 'Highway Star', 'Woman From Tokyo', or 'Child In Time'. I wish the guy good luck. My only thing is, I'm proud of Purple, and just think it would be honest if they were to call themselves something else. Rainbow, or something. That would be fair enough. I think everyone would breathe a sigh of relief. They could go out as Rainbow with dignity and be accepted on a far greater level than if they go out as Deep Purple. But I know *why* they're calling themselves Deep Purple. It looks better on the posters, it's better on the contracts too. They've got a two-million-dollar deal with BMG and I don't know if Rainbow would get a two-million-dollar deal. I think it's a little iffy. Because I'm a fan too. I'm a *great* Deep Purple fan. So I'm disappointed, but I certainly don't wish them any harm. For the sake of Roger, if nothing else, I'd like them to have a successful album, get themselves sorted out, get back on the road again. I have no desire to start a war of words. The end has come and it's great for me, great for them because we don't have to have any more stressful traumas — and it was getting very stressful."

Regarding his comments about the two-million-dollar deal, was Gillan having a casual swipe at Rainbow there, or was he simply making an honest assessment of a business situation? There was a lot of grace and dignity in his comment overall, and so, the latter would perhaps seem more plausible.

With hindsight, Jon Lord was keen to disregard *Slaves And Masters* as a Deep Purple album. In 1994, he went on to tell *Keyboard* that it "was really not a Deep Purple album at all. It carried the name, but the sleeve was deceiving".

Although *Slaves And Masters* was given some good reviews, praising its accessible and melodic songs, it didn't quite match up for everyone who had come to love Purple's heavier sound, or indeed, simply a Gillan-fronted Purple.

Slaves And Masters was plausibly a move forward for Deep Purple after *The House Of Blue Light*. After all, it kept four out of the five Mk2 line-up members working together whilst Turner occupied Gillan's seat for the duration of just one album. That's not in any way intended as a criticism of Joe Lynn Turner, far from it, but the fact is that after *The House Of Blue Light*, if Deep Purple had disbanded entirely to the extent that they had all ended up going their separate ways, then would there have even been any more Deep Purple albums, ever? We'll never know, but it's a consideration that adds weight to the idea that *Slaves And Masters* is an important part of Deep Purple's legacy — even if those who aren't keen on it are to consider it as a simply necessary bridge between *The House Of Blue Light* and *The Battle Rages On...*

Joe Lynn Turner said in March 1991; "Right now Ritchie's playing his ass off 'cause he's re-inspired. Let's face it, for better or for worse, Purple wouldn't have been together if Gillan was still around... Take it from me, nobody in this band is a day at the beach! It's just that Ritchie's the best at it, and everybody else takes lessons from him! Apparently it was obvious with Ian that he was creatively lacking, at least in a Purple direction. The way I heard it — and I got the inside shit — was that it was like that. *The House Of Blue Light* hurt more than anything else. People started to think that the band was going downhill. Let's face it, the credibility's been lost — or at least it's gone downhill — and we've got to fight like bitches to claw our way back up."

A week after the album's release, Steve McCauley — BMG's director of international marketing — said; "*Slaves And Masters* is probably the most musically diverse album that Deep Purple have ever made. We think there are at least four potential hit singles featured on it. It should broaden the appeal of Deep Purple to a wider market than ever before. The aim is to move the music from the exclusively hard rock area into daytime radio airplay. We want to bring back the old fans, as well as win new ones... The first single from the album, 'King Of Dreams', has got off to an amazing start in the US, being picked up by 139 stations in its first week of release, making it the number one most-added track on AOR radio. We expect to get similar support in Europe — and early indications are extremely positive, with stations in Germany, Sweden, Norway and Holland in particular giving 'King Of Dreams' strong support."

Whether or not *Slaves And Masters* succeeded to meet the record company's commercial objectives is open to debate. All the same though, with Joe Lynn Turner on vocals, it made this line-up of Deep Purple similar in sound to the Turner-fronted version of Rainbow. The scope was there to get radio play.

Still though, as many saw it, the record company didn't exactly get what they had signed up for. Well, they sort of did, and they sort of didn't. Polygram had signed Deep Purple MK2 at the time of the 1984 reunion, so technically, they *did* get Deep Purple by name, but was it the Deep Purple that they — and the fans — had been expecting?

Whilst Polygram had been happy with *Perfect Strangers*, they were less impressed with *The House Of Blue Light*. Ultimately, *Nobody's Perfect* was the straw that broke the camel's back. Owing to the fact that it didn't meet their expectations of becoming the definitive live Purple album to replace *Made In Japan*, the label was happy to relinquish the band from its contract.

Matters weren't helped when four months after the release of *Nobody's Perfect*, on his newly-formed label Connoisseur Collection, Tony Edwards released *Scandinavian Nights*. A stellar live concert from a 1970 Swedish radio broadcast, for many older fans, the recording overshadowed those from 1987.

Although the German-based BMG was happy to get Deep Purple Mk2's signatures on a contract, the ink was barely dry when Gillan was given his marching orders, and so, it can't have been the best start for all concerned.

Following the tour in support of *Slaves And Masters*, the band set to work writing new material towards the end of 1991.

Around the same time, although Polygram had been happy to relinquish Purple from its contract, the label released what would become the first of many compilations of material from the two studio albums and the double live.

Initially, two of the jams recorded during the making of *Perfect Strangers* — 'RIJIR' and 'Cosmic Jazz' — were going to be included on *Knocking At Your Back Door: The Best Of Deep Purple In The 80s*. However, for reasons unexplained, they were not. Their inclusion would probably have helped to boost sales, but the two instrumentals remain unreleased to this day.

Many fans were critical of the band for continuing

with a replacement vocalist — specifically in relation to the comments Mk2 had made themselves in 1984 (that the reunion was about Mk2, and if any one of them was to leave, they would call it a day).

To muddy the waters further, whilst the tour with Joe Lynn Turner was in full swing, Tony Edwards released the BBC radio broadcast of the 1985 Knebworth concert. Titled *In The Absence Of Pink*, for many fans, it was a more honest live album compared to *Nobody's Perfect*. With another stark point of comparison made available to the fans, it plausibly didn't do the Turner-fronted Deep Purple any favours.

Over May and June 1992, with Joe Lynn Turner still on vocals, they recorded in studios in New York. They had decided to bring in an outside producer by this point. There had even been talk of bringing Keith Olsen in for the job. On the writing front, the talents of Jim Peterik from Survivor had been considered.

By June 1992, with BMG having signed Mk2 but getting a Turner-fronted Deep Purple, the label was keen to get Gillan back into the band in time for the twenty-fifth anniversary in 1993.

Following the release of *The Battle Rages On...*, Lynn M. Martin — assistant to Bruce Payne — would go on to tell *Music & Media*; "It's good for a band of this status to celebrate its anniversary with a good album, made by what is regarded as its most popular line-up... His [Gillan's] return is very important indeed. The man is very dedicated to the music of Deep Purple. He gave it back its full former identity, and that will certainly make it sell better. The release of *Slaves And Masters* was bad timing. Hard rock was not very popular at that time; rap and dance were taking over. Musically, the album was very different from previous works."

Commercially, the need to have Gillan back was not something that could be glossed over. Colin Hart recalled;

"Bruce wanted to go back for Ian Gillan, but was obviously finding Ritchie a tough one to convince. I don't think he had any argument with Roger, Paicey or Jon."

During June 1992, whilst the record company was making plans to get him back, Gillan was still on tour with his band, and was already scheduled for dates in September. He also had plans to work on a new solo album through to early October, and was on the cusp of launching a new band called Repo Depo.

By some accounts, it was a close call, but the offer to return to Deep Purple was just too good an opportunity to refuse. Colin Hart said; "Apparently, Ian had not had a good time of it away from Purple from a financial point of view, although his latest band Repo Depo was, in his estimation, the real deal and would make it... Once Ian agreed to return in principle, the band dispatched Roger to England with some of the tapes we had recently recorded with Joe for the new album, just to confirm that Ian could still hack it vocally. Nothing could be left to chance, whatever the history."

By August, the backing tracks were close to completion. Work on vocals and lyrics resulted in tracks titled 'Put Your Money Where Your Mouth Is' and 'Bad Business' — a blues style song penned by Glover and Turner.

On Friday 14th August, Joe Lynn Turner left the studio, none the wiser that it would be more than a weekend of time off from Deep Purple. He received a phone call from Bruce Payne telling him that he didn't need to come to work on Monday.

According to Colin Hart, Turner had already sensed that the band wanted Ian Gillan back: "Ritchie stayed silent on the subject, Roger, as always, wanted to get on with the writing, staying away from any controversy. Hard call for him, as he was one of Ian's best chums, but had also served time in Rainbow with Joe very successfully — better to keep the old

Gillan back in Purple?

Negotiations are currently underway with a view to **Ian Gillan** returning to front Deep Purple, following the departure of vocalist Joe Lynn Turner after just one album with the band. Gillan left Deep Purple, amidst much acrimony in 1989, but as next year marks the band's 25th anniversary, it appears that both parties are prepared to make their peace to reform the band's most successful 'Mk. II' line-up in time for the celebrations. While discussions continue, Gillan has been working in the studio on some new solo material.

bandana head down. Bruce needed to bring in reinforcements to finally convince Ritchie that his nemesis Ian should be recalled — the record company. They, I believe, pointed out to him that *Slaves And Masters* had been a relative flop, and if there was to be a renewed enthusiasm for the band from within BMG, then it would be more forthcoming if Gillan was back in the "acceptable" line-up. Ritchie felt that some sort of blame was being placed at his door for the album's failure, never accepting that one of the prime reasons for Ian's departure in the first place, was himself. He reluctantly agreed and Bruce contacted Phil Banfield, who was still Ian's personal manager."

Naturally, it was difficult for Blackmore to welcome Gillan back into the band. He told *Burrn*; "As soon as Joe was gone, everyone began to shout: 'So what now? Looking for another singer again?' In fact, that was my plan. But then Roger Glover said: 'We should get Ian Gillan back, what do you think?' And I said to him: 'I don't want some naked people in front of me again'. Of course Roger defended him by saying: 'That never happened!' I was just joking at the time, but Roger took it very seriously. He didn't get the joke. However: the relationship between myself and Ian Gillan might be very bad, but he is the singer for Deep Purple. When the reunion thing came up in 1984, I was offered to work with David Coverdale, but I refused. Without Ian Gillan, it would have been pointless. Of course, David and Joe are great vocalists. When I hear Gillan's voice on the radio, I always recognise him. And when I hear Joe, it's like 'Is that the singer of Survivor?'. Of course, I love Joe. But he needs some rest now. Maybe it's because of his age, but something was wrong with his voice in the end."

Initially, Blackmore had wanted Mike DiMeo from Riot as the replacement vocalist. "I know him, because I've played football with him," the guitarist recalled, "and he's a very talented singer. But the other guys didn't want him in the band, so that didn't happen."

In his time away from Deep Purple, Gillan had proudly included 'Smoke On The Water' as part of his many live performances. Even away from the band, their repertoire was still very much a part of his identity as a performer. Also, he'd said, "I would dearly love to be singing with Deep Purple now, but I'm doing this and I'll do it with the same commitment as I did all the other things".

All things considered, even with the widely-acknowledged awkwardness between himself and Blackmore, it must have felt good to be back.

The Mk2 line-up spent November and December 1992 getting a majority of material recorded at Red Rooster studios in Tutzing, just outside of Munich. In early 1993, Gillan then went to the Greg Rike studio in Florida, where he put some final sparkle onto the tracks. By late February, everything was ready for mixing, which was done in Los Angeles, and was completed by early March.

Turner had already contributed towards some of the material that would come to feature on *The Battle Rages On...* In an interview for *Burrn*, Blackmore was asked if the keys were changed for Gillan's voice. His response: "I can't remember. I just know that most of the songs sound very different with Ian Gillan."

In earlier meetings with the press, Bruce Payne and Roger Glover had revealed that the new Deep Purple album was going to be called Progress. By 1993 though, the title of *The Battle Rages On...* was confirmed.

One journalist hypothesised that *The Battle Rages On...* had been recorded in many different locations due to the band's personal frictions. Payne's assistant, Lynn M. Martin told *Music & Media*; "It was just different people being at different places at the same time. It didn't have much to do with the so-called bad relationship between Ian and Ritchie, even if saying they can't stand each other isn't far from the truth. The whole operation took about two years, from the first writing of the material until the final recordings."

The album was set for release on the same day everywhere except the US, where a two-week delay had been planned to coincide with a tour there. A single release of 'Anya' — with 'One Man's Meat' on the B-side — was planned for the UK. However, both the UK single and the US tour dates were scrapped. The official reason given for this was that the record company insisted that the album needed to be remixed, which ultimately resulted in a July 1993 release date.

There is much doubt surrounding the official reason as to why the US tour was cancelled. Poor ticket sales is plausibly a stronger likelihood. It is considered by many, that following the forced cancellation of so many shows in 1987, the band had been struggling to engage with an American audience. Also, with many shows having been cancelled in 1991, it appeared that the American audience's appetite for Deep Purple had quickly dissipated.

The launch party for *The Battle Rages On...* took place in London on 22nd July. The album was already on sale in Europe by that point, but became available in UK stores on 26th July. Overall, the album wasn't well advertised. With very little press engagement (and with much negativity when it was there), *The Battle Rages On...* got to number 139 in the US. It's imperative to consider though, that commercially, it wasn't all doom and gloom. The album got to number twenty-one in the UK, as well as hitting the top ten in Japan and handfuls of European countries too.

From Florida's *The Bradenton Herald*: "A better name for *The Battle Rages On...* would be The Once Mighty Band Stumbles On. The same classic Deep Purple line-up responsible for such classic slabs of hard rock as *Deep Purple In Rock* and *Machine Head* was reunited one more time for reasons that *The Battle Rages On...* makes no more clear. This is fairly lame, generic metal stuff, and a song like the concluding 'One Man's Meat' sounds like a *Spinal Tap* reject. Resident guitar god Ritchie Blackmore has a few good riffs left in him, but other than that, there are no victories in this battle."

From Pennsylvania's *The Morning Call*: "One is tempted to now look upon the British band's trailblazing early work as an aberration. *The Battle Rages On...* exhumes the Purps' peak early seventies line-up, which has responded to the challenge with all the verve of a haemorrhoid patient after surgery. It's not just that advanced age has taken its toll — Ian Gillan's operatic howl, in particular, has become an unsatisfying whine. Mostly, it's because the band merely seeks to recast past glories, with guitarist Ritchie Blackmore's overwrought solos and keyboardist Jon Lord's classical pomposity ganging up to make songs such as 'One Man's Meat', 'Nasty Piece Of Work' and 'Solitaire' as refreshing to the ears as a breath of stale air."

Under the heading of "The Ego Battle Rages On", *Music & Media* said; "The Jurassic Park of rock dinosaurs enjoyed a good year of festivities. Jagger has turned fifty. Dinosaur senior Neil Young has just finished his successful European tour, and Deep Purple has celebrated its twenty-fifth anniversary in rock in its classic so-called Mk2 line-up with Ian Gillan as the frontman. The reunion has not escaped radio, and one month before their extensive European tour is taking off. The single, 'Anya', collected playlist reports from twenty-four stations, including major broadcasters. Back in the line-up that made them big in the first place, it won't surprise anybody that the new Deep Purple album — *The Battle Rages On...* — sounds very Purple. Listening to Ritchie Blackmore's inventive guitar riff on the title track, it is as if the years had dissolved. Rhythm tandem bass player Roger Glover (co-producer with

Thom Panunzio) and drummer Ian Paice determine the pace, while Jon Lord further cements the foundation of the classic Purple sound with layers of keyboards. On top of that, there is, of course, singer Ian Gillan, the lost son who — for the second time in his career — re-joins his old mates."

Under the headline of "Purple's Tension Rages On", Ohio's *The Daily Advocate* considered; "This album marks the return of vocalist Ian Gillan, whose firing is frequently cited as the primary reason for Deep Purple's decline over the past few years. Would Gillan's presence really have mattered? He can't quite sing the way he used to, and his last album with Purple, 1988's *Nobody's Perfect*, was an uneven and largely forgettable live effort. Those who shunned Joe Lynn Turner (Gillan's temporary replacement) on 1990's *Slaves And Masters* also forget that the album had several strong cuts (such as 'Fire In The Basement' and 'The Cut Runs Deep'), hence confirming this band's ability to make good music despite personnel changes."

"The latter is one thing that's always separated Deep Purple from the two bands to which it is often compared. Black Sabbath and Led Zeppelin. Save 1983's *Born Again* (which, ironically enough, featured Gillan on lead vocals), Sabbath's membership fluctuations have yielded consistently watered-down versions of the original. When John Bonham died, Zeppelin gave up. The main thing that makes these guys stand out from their fellow legends, however, is their uncanny ability to use internal tension as an impetus for potent songwriting. This was first exhibited in 1969 on the original line-up's last gasp, the criminally underrated *Deep Purple*. It manifested again on the equally underrated *Who Do We Think We Are*, and it's present once more on *The Battle Rages On...*"

"Though there's nothing as killer as 'Child In Time' or 'Smoke On The Water' on this album, it's solid from start to finish. The title track is classic Ritchie Blackmore riffing, and

'Anya' is a nice stretch-out that recalls 'Fools' and 'Flight Of The Rat'. The band even makes the much-overused Peter Gunn riff work on 'Nasty Piece Of Work'. Hard to believe, but this is five men hitting middle age playing as if it's their first album. Is Deep Purple to heavy metal what James Brown is to soul? This album has cinched that analogy."

The *Indiana Gazette* considered; "*The Battle Rages On...* makes no concessions to what's going on in music now. It's not grunge, it's not heavy metal — it's just Deep Purple being Deep Purple. The band made its fortune on Blackmore's dark, dramatic guitar, undercut by the keening of Lord's various keyboards (particularly his trademark Hammond B-3 organ) and topped off by Gillan's unmistakable wails. The formula is still intact."

Some saw *The Battle Rages On...* as an opportunity to get away from the musical stylings that had been predominant on *Slaves And Masters*. Jon Lord told *Keyboard*; "I had the feeling that we had to prove something with the new album (*The Battle Rages On...*). We had said to ourselves that when we were to record an album for our twenty-fifth anniversary, it had to be a real Deep Purple album, not some surrogate Deep Purple album like *Slaves And Masters*."

There was perhaps also a sense that Mk2 was under pressure to live up to the legend of their past. Gillan told a journalist in 1993, "Those guys are fantastic musicians. Sometimes that can be a sort of lead weight around your neck because you're living up to expectations and history. I think objectives and reputations have been the downfall of Deep Purple over the years. When we had no objectives and we just did what comes naturally have been the times when we've produced the best stuff, and I think that's pretty much what happened this time."

Following some rehearsals in Bregenz, Austria on 21st September 1993, the tour kicked off in Italy, where the band had a full on-stage rehearsal on the 23rd and performed their first official show on 24th.

Although the band's rapport wasn't great around this time, there was no denying that the tension had its uses for the purpose of performance. Blackmore said, "Although none of us will ever be the best of friends off stage, it's an explosive gelling of individuals, which hits the button on stage and on record."

"Most of the difficulties have always been between Ritchie and myself," said Gillan. "I've probably been more trouble than anyone in this band... I look at Purple as an ex-wife. We got married in '69 and divorced in '73, then we got married again in '84 and divorced again in '89. I made my mind up I was never gonna marry that woman ever again. But from time to time, I think it's pretty cool to meet up in a sleazy hotel and have a wild affair."

"The chemistry within Deep Purple is absolutely spectacular, sometimes to the point of demolition," he said. "I think probably there are moments where it's so intense that it's either wonderful or horrendous. We've been very good at times. We've been terrible at other times. I think we've made a good effort over the years. I look back with great pride at having worked with great players."

Birmingham's *Evening Mail* reported on 9th November 1993; "Rock legends Deep Purple are back in action tonight at the NEC on the final date of their twenty-fifth anniversary tour. It's a *Mail Live!* special and possibly the last chance to see the original Mk2 line-up. My pop pal Graham Young caught up with them at Manchester Apollo on Friday night to get a sneak preview of the set, and he tells me that the lads were really cooking in a stunning two-hour set featuring the full laser show they bought on tour in 1987."

"But the well-documented problems between singer Gillan and guitarist Blackmore seem to be continuing. At the

Lord saves the day

POP REVIEWS

Deep Purple
NEC Arena

DINOSAURS ruled the earth again as Deep Purple came back to town with their greatest line-up. It was like being in *The Land That Time Forgot*.

It had taken their 25th anniversary to get singer Ian Gillan back into the fold — and it showed.

Guitarist Ritchie Blackmore was missing for the first third of opener *Highway Star* and it was almost a case of 'Will he or won't he?'

But ace keyboardsman Jon Lord, the most underrated rock star on earth, was there to save the day.

Given their differences, it's astonishing they can still write quality songs like *The Battle Rages On* and *Anya*, which fitted perfectly with established classics like *Child In Time* and *Smoke On The Water*.

Gillan looked in great shape, too, but with Blackmore's ego tempered by the singer's return, fans didn't quite get the collective performance that they deserved. Or, indeed, any news as to whether this memorable night, which was filmed, would go down in history as Purple's last British gig.

GRAHAM YOUNG

Apollo, the pair didn't acknowledge each other throughout the entire show — and at the end, there was again more evidence of that ill feeling. Blackmore left the stage alone, while Gillan marched off in the opposite direction with the rest of the band. A few tickets are still available for tonight's gig. Miss it and you miss a piece of living rock history."

On 9th November, Deep Purple's performance at Birmingham's NEC Arena was recorded (it would appear on the 1994 video and CD release, *Come Hell Or High Water*). Under the headline of "Lord Saves The Day", a British newspaper reported: "Deep Purple, NEC Arena. Dinosaurs ruled the earth again as Deep Purple came back to town with their greatest line-up. It was like being in *The Land That Time Forgot*. It had taken their twenty-fifth anniversary to get singer Ian Gillan back into the fold, and it showed. Guitarist Ritchie Blackmore was missing for the first third of opener 'Highway Star' and it was almost a case of 'will he or won't he?'. But ace keyboards man Jon Lord, the most underrated rock star on Earth, was there to save the day."

"Given their differences, it's astonishing they can still write quality songs like 'The Battle Rages On...' and 'Anya', which fitted perfectly with established classics like 'Child In Time' and 'Smoke On The Water'. Gillan looked in great shape too, but with Blackmore's ego tempered by the singer's return, fans didn't quite get the collective performance that they deserved. Or, indeed, any news as to whether this memorable night, which was filmed, will go down in history as Purple's last British gig."

Having famously referred to Deep Purple's 1993 album as "The Cattle Grazes On", by 30th October, Blackmore had handed in his resignation. It was unsurprising to some. Having seen the extensive tour plan that never came to fruition, a British journalist had said in July 1993; "Further dates are also being lined up in Australia, Japan and other Far Eastern countries for 1994. That's an awful lot of touring for a band who don't get on!".

And as another journalist had rightly considered prior to Blackmore's exit, "Group members have seen more upheaval and infighting" than "most bands would put up with without completely calling it quits".

In response to Blackmore leaving the band, BMG issued a press release on 17th November 1993. The news divided fan opinion, with some considering that his live performances had been subpar around that time anyway. Others insisted that without Blackmore, it was all over for Deep Purple.

Just weeks prior to Blackmore's departure from Deep Purple, what was said in the build-up to the event indicates that it wasn't a foregone conclusion that the guitarist would be the one to go. For indeed, Gillan was seemingly cautious to invest too heavily in Deep Purple what with everything that *he* had experienced. "I'm a writer and a singer," he said. "I don't feel I can serve Purple, or anyone, really, just by sitting around waiting for two years until the next album's going to be together. I'm very defensive about giving my heart to Deep Purple at the moment. I don't feel that I want to place my trust in something that has been wounding so many times. I think it's fair to say that I'm going into it in a fairly guarded way, and so far, so good… If I can have any ambition at all, it won't be too much of a long-term thing. If we can finish the tour without ripping each other to pieces, then I think Purple will have regained a bit of dignity, a bit of confidence, and a bit of self-respect."

Following Blackmore's departure, Deep Purple were due to perform in Japan. It was a tremendous relief for all concerned when Joe Satriani agreed to fill in on guitar. With the Japanese crowds hungry to see Blackmore, it was imperative that Deep Purple had a replacement who could get them just as fired-up. Luckily, Satriani already had a strong following

Perfect Strangers - *Deep Purple 1984-1993*

VI ØNSKER DEEP PURPLE VELKOMMEN TIL NORGE!

Gå ikke glipp av den legendariske original-
besetningen bestående av Ian Gillan, Ritchie
Blackmore, Roger Glover, Jon Lord og Ian
Paice, som i kveld inntar Oslo Spektrum's
scene med et forrykende live-show!

Ny CD & kassett
«THE BATTLE RAGES ON»
Inkl. den rykende ferske singlen «Time To Kill»

I SALG NÅ!

there. Not only that, but he was quickly able to adapt and take on the Deep Purple setlist, so much so that time set aside for rehearsals didn't need to be utilised. Satriani had done his homework to the extent that he played guitar parts that the rest of the band hadn't heard in a while.

In the interest of transparency, prior to the shows in Japan, fans were informed that Blackmore would not be performing, and that they could get a refund as a result of that. Despite this, the number of people demanding a refund was a relatively small proportion of ticket holders.

With Gillan back in Deep Purple, it is hardly surprising that Blackmore's time with the band wasn't looking like a sustainable prospect. There was little interaction between the pair, as Blackmore explained; "We almost don't communicate. When we talk, it's just little things. When we sit down together at the table, Ian always sits far away from me. Our communication is very limited. It's like: 'Ian, how are you?' 'Thank you, all is well'. We are like two tigers in one cage. But we managed to do this record somehow. I think we both respect each other, but Ian is not interested in me as a person and vice-versa. But when we get on stage, everything changes. He knows how to make me laugh on stage, but overall, for me, Ian is a very boring person. I don't really know how to describe him. Perhaps he could be called a "rebel soul". We are both very quarrelsome, since our school days. But he uses his aggressions in his lyrics and his singing. I'm a little bit different in that aspect. However, I will never forget this one joke he did on stage in Japan, I think. He was introducing 'Perfect Strangers' and said: 'The next song is dedicated to the football team, Perfect Street Rangers'... But the funniest thing happened afterwards. He said: 'That was a song called Perfect Street Rangers, and the next one is about...'. We all thought: 'What is he talking about again now?'. Every time we finished playing a song, Ian Paice and Jon had to explain what

Ian was joking about, because Roger always took it a little bit too serious. We are united by one thing. We both hate the show business side. When journalists start treating Ian Gillan too seriously, he's always giving weird answers. He likes to give interviews in good company, because there are many journalists who are just rude and asking corny stuff, so he just gives them "nonsense" answers, but with a serious facial expression. I like that dry humour. Paicey, Roger and Jon are not into that. If you want to read the most boring interview, then read an interview with Roger Glover. Of course he likes to joke too. But in a very strange way."

There was certainly the use of humour to carry things through, but that alone clearly wasn't enough. The tensions were high during the tour of *The Battle Rages On...*, as is well documented in the 2019 book, *A Nasty Piece Of Work* by Jerry Bloom.

Blackmore was pretty candid about the tensions surrounding *The Battle Rages On...* even before the problems reached a point that saw him leave the band: "At first that song was called 'Vicious Circle'. But then Ian finished the lyrics and called it 'The Battle Rages On...'. I've found that it was a very strong name, and I said to Bruce, 'Let's call the album that too'. Bruce started laughing and said that this name perfectly reflects the relationships within the group. I've used the riff for that song already a few years ago in Rainbow."

The Rainbow song in question is 'Fire Dance'. "But it was much faster," said Blackmore. "I really like this riff and I played it to Jon, I think. And Jon said, 'That's a good riff, fits the song perfectly'. And then I told him that I've already used it in one of my earlier songs, but he said, 'There is nothing wrong about playing things you've written yourself'. And so the song was born. I think it worked very well within the context of the song. But I have to admit that I haven't heard the album. Well, maybe I should give it a listen — at some later stage, if I'm not busy looking out of the window and I'm in the right mood."

After calling it a day with Deep Purple, Blackmore made one more Rainbow album in 1995 — *Stranger In Us All* — with a whole new line-up including Doogie White on vocals. During the tour for the album, the setlist included Purple songs from both Mk2.1 ('Black Night', 'Smoke On The Water' and 'Burn') and Mk2.2 ('Perfect Strangers'). Thereafter, he turned his back on rock music to focus on his new project, Blackmore's Night. It wasn't until 2015 that he began getting a new line-up of Rainbow together — with Ronnie Romero as vocalist — for the purpose of touring.

In 2016, Deep Purple was inducted into the Rock 'n' Roll Hall Of Fame, and whilst this included Blackmore, he didn't attend the ceremony. His reasons are known only to himself, but based on the fact that he has avoided many publicity gatherings throughout his career — whether with Deep Purple or Rainbow — it would perhaps be excessive to assume that his non-attendance was done as a snub towards Deep Purple itself. We'll never know.

It would also be excessive to consider that following Blackmore's departure from the band, the future of Deep Purple was set to be in ruins. For of course, following all the dramas of 1993, across several different line-ups, Deep Purple has been going strong since, and continues to do so to this very day. At the time of writing this book, a line-up of nucleus Ian Gillan, Roger Glover and Ian Paice are on tour with Don Airey on keyboards, and Simon McBride on guitar (Airey officially replaced Jon Lord in 2002, and in 2022, McBride took over from Steve Morse — a valued member of Deep Purple from 1994 to 2022). Their presence is much to the joy of many fans who missed out on live performances due to the Covid-19 pandemic, and indeed, who are just happy to see one of their favourite bands still going.

Considering that prior to the Mk2 reunion in 1984, Deep Purple hadn't been going in any official form since 1976, it could be said that, for better or worse, it was this reunion that ignited the flame that is still carried on the torch of Deep Purple to this day. If the 1984 reunion only had value in that sense, then really, it can't be a bad thing.

So was the 1984 reunion a good idea? Overall, the answer is arguably a resounding yes. Despite some cynicism from some fans and the music press, Deep Purple Mk2 were incredibly successful with their tour for the *Perfect Strangers* album, and indeed, the album itself generally fared well in most reviews. Of course there were some who felt that it didn't hit the mark compared to Mk2's seventies output, but really, such criticisms were inevitable considering the expectation on the legend of Deep Purple.

Taking that out of the equation, *Perfect Strangers* did well commercially not just in and of itself, but in terms of how it was an anomaly in comparison to the genres of music that were more predominant in popular music charts at the time. Impressively, this was the case globally.

Not only that, but even in the category of rock music, at the time of the reunion, Deep Purple were thought of as uncool by some; their image and their sound certainly didn't match that of the hair metal and thrash that was being championed at the time (that said, publications such as *Kerrang!* and *Metal Hammer* were generally supportive of the Mk2 reunion throughout the entirety of that line-up's tenure. For indeed, anyone who knows their rock music would be doing themselves a disservice in choosing to dismiss Deep Purple as irrelevant).

From the point of view of the band, 1984 and 1985 were good years for them. Not only is *Perfect Strangers* and the tour that supported it demonstrative of this, but also, everyone spoke so positively in interviews of how happy they were to be back in Deep Purple — of how right it felt and how it was more than just a flash-in-the-pan thing.

With hindsight in mind, it is evident that none of the band members were simply waxing lyrical for the sake of promotional purposes there, for by 1983, every member of the Mk2 line-up was, to at least some extent, in limbo with their careers.

In 1983, even with the biggest success story being Rainbow, even Blackmore and Glover had itchy feet. As for Ian Paice, Jon Lord and Ian Gillan, based on where their careers were at commercially and creatively around that time, to be back in the Purple fold was surely a step up by any stretch of the imagination (and that's not to disrespect the work that Paice and Lord did with Whitesnake, or what Gillan did with Black Sabbath; it's just that as members of Deep Purple, the three of them were in a better position to contribute creatively and to reap the rewards commercially. Deep Purple was, after all, *their* band).

With the advantage of hindsight, it could be considered that following the success of the *Perfect Strangers* album and tour, perhaps Mk2 would have done themselves a favour to have called it a day there and then.

"*Perfect Strangers* — I thought that was a very good record. Then the second one (*The House Of Blue Light*), I thought that was really bad," said Blackmore in 2013. "At the time, people thought we'd only stay together for one record. After that second one, maybe we should have called it a day, although, I really liked *Slaves And Masters* with Joe Lynn Turner. But again, I'm heavy into melody. A lot of people didn't like it simply because it was him, which I always found strange."

It is abundantly clear that when it came to making *The House Of Blue Light* and *The Battle Rages On...*, on the whole, the Mk2 line-up were not happy campers. The fact that it took everyone a while to get it together to make those albums is demonstrative of that.

From a fan perspective, the fact that Deep Purple Mk2 carried on for those two albums and resulting tours is, overall, a positive. It spawned more music and, as much as the live album *Nobody's Perfect* got mixed reviews and divided opinion amongst fans, bootlegs from the entirety of Mk2's reunion tenure show that if you take the behind-the-scenes politics out of the equation, the band were playing incredibly well together on stage and making some damn good music. In that sense, to look at the entirety of the Mk2 reunion as an outsider, the term "no regrets" springs to mind.

So, the Mk2 years covering 1984 to 1993: Was it a good idea, and does the music it resulted in still hold weight to this day? It's a question that will always divide opinion for a long time to come. It perhaps also depends on what each individual fan's experience is.

For instance, the reunion enabled a younger generation of fans to see Mk2 performing live, but for older fans who got to see the band in the seventies, the excitement and overall feeling might not have been quite the same. Me personally, I wasn't around in the seventies and was still very much into my nursery rhyme cassettes by 1993. As a result, as someone who can look at the Mk2 reunion from a wholly retrospective point of view, I'm all for it.

Discography

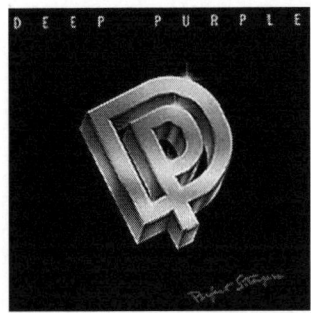

Perfect Strangers (1984)
All songs by Ritchie Blackmore, Ian Gillan and Roger Glover except where noted.

'Son Of Alerik' had appeared in an edited form on the 7" B-side of the 'Perfect Strangers' single, and in full on the 12" 'Perfect Strangers' single and the European version of the compilation, *Knocking At Your Back Door: The Best Of Deep Purple In The 80s.*

Side One
1. Knocking At Your Back Door (7:09)
2. Under The Gun (4:40)
3. Nobody's Home (Blackmore, Gillan, Glover, Lord, Paice) (4:01)
4. Mean Streak (4:26)

Side Two
5. Perfect Strangers (5:31)
6. A Gypsy's Kiss (4:14)
7. Wasted Sunsets (3:58)
8. Hungry Daze (5:01)

Cassette and CD release extra track:
9. Not Responsible (4:53)

1999 CD bonus track:
10. Son Of Alerik (Blackmore) (10:01)

Production
Produced by Roger Glover and Deep Purple
Recorded at Horizons, Stowe, Vermont with Le Mobile Studio, 1984
Mixed at Tennessee Tonstudio, Hamburg, Germany
Engineered by Nick Blagona
Mastered by Greg Calbi at Sterling Sound, New York

The House Of Blue Light (1987)
All tracks written by Ritchie Blackmore, Ian Gillan and Roger Glover, except where noted.

Side One
1. Bad Attitude (Blackmore, Gillan, Glover, Lord) (4:32)
2. The Unwritten Law (Blackmore, Gillan, Glover, Paice) (4:34)
3. Call Of The Wild (Gillan, Blackmore, Glover, Lord) (4:48)
4. Mad Dog (4:29)
5. Black & White (Blackmore, Gillan, Glover, Lord) (3:39)

Side Two
6. Hard Lovin' Woman (3:25)
7. The Spanish Archer (4:56)
8. Strangeways (5:56)
9. Mitzi Dupree (5:05)
10. Dead Or Alive (4:42)

Production
Produced by Roger Glover and Deep Purple
Recorded at the Playhouse, Stowe, Vermont, with Le Mobile operated by Guy Charbonneau
Engineered by Nick Blagona
Mixed by Harry Schnitzler at Union Studios, Munich, West Germany
Mastered by Greg Calbi at Sterling Sound, New York

Discography

Nobody's Perfect (1988)

Some of the tracks are not necessarily included in every existing edition of the album. The original 1988 double LP release has thirteen tracks, omitting 'Dead Or Alive'. The 1988 cassette version includes 'Dead Or Alive', but omits 'Bad Attitude'. The first one-disc CD edition from 1988 consists of just eleven tracks, leaving out both and also 'Space Truckin''. Finally, all the indicated tracks were included on the 1999 double CD remaster.

All tracks are written by Ritchie Blackmore, Ian Gillan, Roger Glover, Jon Lord and Ian Paice, except where noted. All recording locations and dates noted in brackets.

Disc One
1. Highway Star (Irvine Meadows, California on 23rd May 1987) (6:10)
2. Strange Kind Of Woman (Irvine Meadows, California on 23rd May 1987) (7:34)
3. Dead Or Alive (Blackmore, Gillan, Glover) (Milan, Italy on 4th September 1987) (7:05)
4. Perfect Strangers (Blackmore, Gillan, Glover) (Irvine Meadows, California on 23rd May 1987) (6:25)
5. Hard Lovin' Woman (Blackmore, Gillan, Glover) (Oslo, Norway on 22nd August 1987) (5:03)
6. Bad Attitude (Blackmore, Gillan, Glover, Lord) (Phoenix, Arizona on 30th May 1987) (5:30)
7. Knocking At Your Back Door (Blackmore, Gillan, Glover) (Phoenix, Arizona on 30th May 1987) (11:24)

Disc Two
1. Child In Time (Phoenix, Arizona on 30th May 1987 and Oslo, Norway on 22nd August 1987) (10:36)
2. Lazy (Phoenix, Arizona on 30th May 1987) (5:10)
3. Space Truckin' (Oslo, Norway on 22nd August 1987) (6:03)
4. Black Night (Verona, Italy on 6th September 1987 and Oslo, Norway on 22nd August 1987) (6:06)
5. Woman From Tokyo (Irvine Meadows, California on 23rd May 1987) (4:00)
6. Smoke On The Water (Oslo, Norway on 22nd August 1987) (7:46)
7. Hush (Joe South) (Live Jam at Hook End Manor on 26th February 1988) (3:32)

Production
Produced by Roger Glover and Deep Purple
Mixed at Outside Studios, Hook End Manor, England, 11th February — 16th March 1988
Engineered by Nick Davis
Assistant engineer: Simon Metcalfe

The Battle Rages On... (1993)
All tracks are written by Ritchie Blackmore, Ian Gillan and Roger Glover, except where noted.

Side One
1. The Battle Rages On... (Blackmore, Gillan, Lord, Paice) (5:56)
2. Lick It Up (3:59)
3. Anya (Blackmore, Gillan, Glover, Lord) (6:32)
4. Talk About Love (4:11)
5. Time To Kill (5:49)

Side Two
6. Ramshackle Man (5:34)
7. A Twist In The Tale (4:17)
8. Nasty Piece Of Work (Blackmore, Gillan, Glover, Lord) (4:43)
9. Solitaire (4:42)
10. One Man's Meat (4:38)

Production
Produced by Thom Panunzio and Roger Glover
Basic tracks produced by Thom Panunzio at Bearsville Studios in upstate New York (engineered by Bill Kennedy, assisted by Mike Reiter)
Vocals and overdubs recorded at Red Rooster Studios (engineered by Hans Gemperle) in Tutzing, Germany, and Greg Rike Studios (engineered by Jason Corsaro, assisted by Wally Walton and Darren Schneider) in Orlando, Florida.
Mixed by Pat Regan with Roger Glover at Sound on Sound Recording (engineered by Pat Regan, assisted by John Siket, Devin Emke and Peter Beckeman) in New York, and at the Ambient Recording Company (engineered by Pat Regan, assisted by Mark Conese) in Connecticut
Mastered by George Marino at Sterling Sound in New York.

Discography

Come Hell Or High Water (1994)
All songs written by Ritchie Blackmore, Ian Gillan, Roger Glover, Jon Lord and Ian Paice except where noted.

1. Highway Star (6:40)
2. Black Night (5:40)
3. A Twist In The Tale (Blackmore, Gillan, Glover) (4:27)
4. Perfect Strangers (Blackmore, Gillan, Glover) (6:52)
5. Anyone's Daughter (3:57)
6. Child In Time (10:48)
7. Anya (Blackmore, Gillan, Glover, Lord) (12:13)
8. Speed King (7:29)
9. Smoke On The Water (10:26)

Production
Produced, engineered and mixed by Pat Regan at New Century Media Studios, Los Angeles
Mastered by George Marino at Sterling Sound, New York.

Singles

1984	Knocking At Your Back Door / Wasted Sunsets
	Most territories except UK.
1984	Knocking At Your Back Door / Son Of Alerik
	Canadian 12".
1985	Perfect Strangers / Son Of Alerik
1985	Knocking At Your Back Door / Perfect Strangers
1987	Call Of The Wild / Dead Or Alive
1987	Call Of The Wild / Strangeways
1987	Bad Attitude / Black & White
1988	Hush, Dead Or Alive (live) / Bad Attitude (live)*
	*Extra track on 12".
1993	Anya / One Man's Meat
	Germany and Japan only.
1993	Time To Kill / Nasty Piece Of Work
1994	Anyone's Daughter (live) / Speed King (live)

Discography

Retrospective Releases

Compared to the vast amount of retrospective releases of Mk2 material from the 1969-73 period, there is relatively little from the '84-'93 period. This is partly because the band's original management team of Tony Edwards and John Coletta controlled the earlier material through HEC Enterprises and were happy to licence it around the world, whereas when Bruce Payne brokered the deals in 1984 with Polygram and 1989 with BMG, the record companies retained control and have been far less proactive.

Some might also argue that the demand for live releases of the reunion period isn't quite as strong as it is for what many still see as the halcyon days of the seventies.

Furthermore, with the band continuing after Blackmore's departure, there appears to be little appetite for agreeing to release recordings from the Mk2 reunion period.

That said, Universal began preparing to revamp the catalogue in 2011 with deluxe editions of *Perfect Strangers* and *The House Of Blue Light*, but to date, these have remained on the back burner.

In The Absence Of Pink – Knebworth '85 (1991)

The BBC recording of the one and only British show from the Perfect Strangers tour. Neither 'Under The Gun' nor 'Woman From Tokyo' were broadcasted and were thus not included.

In 2018, Universal prepared advanced listening copies of a reissue — complete with 'Under The Gun' and 'Woman From Tokyo' — but it still hasn't materialised.

The Bootleg Series 1984 – 2000 (2000)

A 12-CD box set that adopted the approach made popular by other artists of officially releasing exact replicas of bootlegs. All are double CDs of gigs from 1984.

CDs 1/2 **Highway Stars**
(Memorial Drive, Adelaide, Australia. November 30th 1984)
CDs 3/4 **Third Night**
(Johanneshov Isstadion, Stockholm June 16th 1985)
CDs 5/6 **Hungary Days**
(Budapest, Hungary, January 26/27/28th 1987)
CDs 7/8 **In Your Trousers**
(Stockholm, November 13th 1993)
The remaining two in the set are from the Steve Morse era of the band.

Live In Europe 1993 (2006)
A 4-CD box set containing the full shows for Stuttgart and Birmingham that were used for the *Come Hell Or High Water* release. There were numerous pressing issues with the early batches; the Stuttgart gig was on discs labelled NEC, and vice versa. On some copies, the Stuttgart first disc is missing and the NEC first disc is duplicated.

Live In Stuttgart (2007)
Live At The NEC 1993 (2007)
Both shows from the *Live In Europe* box set were released independently as double CDs.

Perfect Strangers Live (2013)
Recorded in Sydney, 12th December 1984. Released in multiple formats as a concert video on DVD and audio CD and LP formats. In order to fit the gig onto two LPs, 'Child In Time' is edited to less than five minutes, using only the second part of the performance after the guitar solo.

Ward Records in Japan issued a box set combining all three formats. The vinyl was spread across three LPs and has no edits.

The DVD also includes a twenty-three-minute mini-documentary with previously unreleased footage from the *Perfect Strangers* rehearsals.

Compilation albums

Despite Polygram only releasing three Mk2 albums between 1984-88, they have continued to put out compilations of the material at alarming regularity.

Likewise, BMG Sony, who got the bum end of the deal with three different line-ups across three studio albums, plus the Mk2 1994 live album, have also released several compilations, each one combining material from all three line-ups. The BMG releases are indicated with*.

Knocking At Your Back Door: The Best Of Deep Purple In The 80s (1991)
Progression (also released as **Rock Giants**) (1993)
Hush (1993)
Child In Time (1995)
Best II – Child In Time (1996)
Knocking At Your Back Door (1997)
Essential Rock (1997)
South African only release.
Smoke On The Water (1998)
Purplexed (1998)*
Under The Gun (1999)
Classic Deep Purple –The Universal Masters Collection (2003)
Reissued as The Colour Collection, 2006.
Winning Combinations (2003)
Includes both Deep Purple and Rainbow tracks.
1990-1996 (2004)*
Speed King – The Fastest Tracks (2005)*
The Collection (2006)*
Hit Collection (2007)*
Gold – Greatest Hits – 3-CD Set (2009)*
Icon (2012)

Perfect Strangers - *Deep Purple 1984-1993*

Tour Dates

The 1984-85 Perfect Strangers tour was extensive and hugely successful. The 1987 House Of Blue Light tour was also commercially successful. After Blackmore's broken finger necessitated the cancelling of the remaining US dates, the band's popularity never really recovered in the States.

It is also worth noting that overall, the reformed Mk2 only played ten shows in the United Kingdom.

1984

-- September — Night Club One, Hamburg, Germany
Impromptu gig as a four-piece because there were no keyboards in the club.

27th November	Entertainment Centre, Perth, Australia
30th November	Memorial Drive, Adelaide, Australia
1st December	Western Springs, Auckland, New Zealand
2nd December	Western Springs, Auckland, New Zealand
4th December	Athletic Park, Wellington, New Zealand
5th December	Bruce Indoor Stadium, Canberra, Australia
7th December	QE II Park, Christchurch, New Zealand
9th December	Festival Hall, Brisbane, Australia
10th December	Festival Hall, Brisbane, Australia
12th December	Entertainment Centre, Sydney, Australia
13th December	Entertainment Centre, Sydney, Australia
14th December	Entertainment Centre, Sydney, Australia
16th December	Entertainment Centre, Melbourne, Australia
17th December	Entertainment Centre, Melbourne, Australia
18th December	Entertainment Centre, Melbourne, Australia

1985

18th January	Ector County Coliseum Odessa, Texas, USA
19th January	Civic Centre, Amarillo, Texas, USA
20th January	Coliseum-Britt Brown Arena, Wichita, Kansas, USA
24th January	Summit, Houston, Texas, USA
25th January	Reunion Arena, Dallas, Texas, USA
26th January	Convention Centre Arena, San Antonio, Texas, USA
28th January	County Coliseum, El Paso, Texas, USA
31st January	Cow Palace, Daly City, California, USA
1st February	Long Beach Arena, Los Angeles, California, USA
2nd February	Long Beach Arena, Los Angeles, California, USA
4th February	Veterans Memorial Coliseum, Phoenix, Arizona, USA
5th February	Sports Arena, San Diego, California, USA
7th February	Tingley Coliseum, Albuquerque, New Mexico, USA
8th February	McNichols Arena, Denver, Colorado, USA *Originally scheduled for the Coliseum, 9th February*
12th February	Kiel Auditorium, St Louis, Missouri, USA
13th February	Kemper Arena, Kansas City, Missouri, USA
15th February	Met Centre, Bloomington, Minnesota, USA
16th February	UIC Pavilion, Chicago, Illinois, USA
17th February	UIC Pavilion, Chicago, Illinois, USA
19th February	Joe Louis Arena, Detroit, Michigan, USA
20th February	The Coliseum, Cleveland, Ohio, USA
21st February	The Coliseum, Cleveland, Ohio, USA
23rd February	The Spectrum, Philadelphia, Pennsylvania, USA
24th February	Civic Arena, Pittsburgh, Pennsylvania, USA
26th February	Vets. Memorial Coliseum, New Haven, Connecticut, USA
28th February	Centrum Worcester, Massachusetts, USA
2nd March	Centrum Worcester, Massachusetts, USA
3rd March	Centrum Worcester, Massachusetts, USA
4th March	Civic Centre, Providence, Rhode Island, USA
5th March	Civic Centre, Providence, Rhode Island, USA
9th March	East Rutherford, Meadowlands Arena, New Jersey, USA
11th March	Joe Louis Arena, Detroit, Michigan, USA
12th March	Cincinnati Gardens, Ohio, USA

Tour Dates

13th March	Market Square Arena, Indianapolis, Indiana, USA
15th March	Coliseum, Jacksonville, Florida, USA
16th March	Sportatorium, Hollywood, Florida, USA
17th March	Civic Centre Arena, Lakeland, Florida, USA
20th March	New York, USA (unconfirmed)
25th March	Meadowlands Arena, East Rutherford, New Jersey, USA *Originally scheduled for Toronto, postponed to 1st April*
26th March	The Spectrum, Philadelphia, Pennsylvania, USA
28th March	Civic Centre Arena, Ottawa, Ontario, Canada
29th March	Colisée de Québec, Quebec, Canada
31st March	Forum, Montreal, Quebec, Canada
1st April	Maple Leaf Gardens, Toronto, Ontario, Canada
3rd April	Civic Centre Arena, St. Paul, Minnesota, USA
6th April	Coliseum Concert Bowl, Vancouver, British Columbia, Canada
8th April	Memorial Coliseum, Portland, Oregon, USA
9th April	Tacoma Dome, Seattle, Washington, USA
3rd May	NBC Arena, Honolulu, Hawaii, USA
8th May	Jo Hall, Osaka, Japan
9th May	Jo Hall, Osaka, Japan
11th May	International Exhibition Hall, Nagoya, Japan
13th May	Budokan, Tokyo, Japan
14th May	Budokan, Tokyo, Japan
15th May	Budokan, Tokyo, Japan
16th May	Budokan, Tokyo, Japan
14th June	Isstadion, Stockholm, Sweden
15th June	Isstadion, Stockholm, Sweden
16th June	Isstadion, Stockholm, Sweden
18th June	Isstadion, Malmö, Sweden
22nd June	Knebworth Park, Knebworth, England
24th June	Limburghal, Genk, Belgium
26th June	Stadthalle Vienna, Austria
27th June	Stadthalle Vienna, Austria
29th June	Maimarktgelände, Mannheim, Germany
30th June	Rot-Weiß-Sportplatz, Frankfurt/Main, Germany
2nd July	Estadio del Rayo Vallecano, Madrid, Spain *Postponed to 17th July*

Perfect Strangers - *Deep Purple 1984-1993*

3rd July	Estadio Narcis Sala (C.F. San Andres), Barcelona, Spain *Postponed to 16th July*
6th July	Zeppelinfeld, Nürnberg, Germany
8th July	Palais Omnisports de Paris-Bercy, Paris, France
9th July	Palais Omnisports de Paris-Bercy, Paris, France
11th July	Stade De L'Ouest, Nice, France
13th July	Hallenstadion, Zürich, Switzerland
14th July	Hallenstadion, Zürich, Switzerland
15th July	Stadio Comunale, Turin, Italy
16th July	Estadio Narcis Sala (C.F. San Andres), Barcelona, Spain *Rescheduled from 3rd July*
17th July	Estadio del Rayo Vallecano, Madrid, Spain *Rescheduled from 2nd July*
14th August	Merriweather Post Pavilion, Columbia, Maryland, USA
15th August	Convention Centre, Niagara Falls, New York, USA
17th August	Alpine Valley Music Theatre, East Troy, Wisconsin, USA
18th August	Atwood Stadium, Flint, Michigan, USA
20th August	Community War Memorial, Rochester, New York, USA
24th August	Cotton Bowl, Dallas, Texas, USA

Tour Dates

1987

26th January	Sportcsarnok, Budapest, Hungary
27th January	Sportcsarnok, Budapest, Hungary
28th January	Sportcsarnok, Budapest, Hungary
31st January	Weser-Ems-Halle, Oldenburg, Germany
1st February	Messehalle, Hannover, Germany
3rd February	Deutschlandhalle, Berlin, Germany
4th February	Westfalenhalle, Dortmund, Germany
6th February	Saarlandhalle, Saarbrücken, Germany
8th February	Sporthalle, Köln, Germany
9th February	Festhalle, Frankfurt/Main, Germany
11th February	Rhein-Neckar-Halle, Eppelheim, Germany
13th February	Palatrussardi, Milan, Italy
14th February	Hallenstadion, Zürich, Switzerland
15th February	Hallenstadion, Zürich, Switzerland
17th February	Olympiahalle, München, Germany
18th February	Hanns-Martin-Schleyer-Halle, Stuttgart, Germany
20th February	Palais Omnisports de Paris-Bercy, Paris, France
21st February	Vorst National, Brussels, Belgium
22nd February	Ahoy, Rotterdam, Netherlands
23rd February	Ahoy, Rotterdam, Netherlands
25th February	Isstadion, Malmö, Sweden
27th February	Isstadion, Stockholm, Sweden
28th February	Scandinavium, Gothenburg, Sweden
3rd March	Wembley Arena, London, England
4th March	Wembley Arena, London, England
6th March	The Playhouse, Edinburgh, Scotland
7th March	NEC, Birmingham, England
8th March	NEC, Birmingham, England
15th April	Forum, Montreal, Quebec, Canada
16th April	Cumberland County Civic Centre, Portland, Maine, USA
17th April	Civic Centre, Hartford, Connecticut, USA
18th April	Community War Memorial, Rochester, New York, USA
21st April	Centrum, Worcester, Massachusetts, USA
22nd April	Centrum, Worcester, Massachusetts, USA *Rescheduled from 20th April*

Perfect Strangers - *Deep Purple 1984-1993*

23rd April	Civic Centre, Providence, Rhode Island, USA
24th April	The Spectrum, Philadelphia, Pennsylvania, USA
25th April	The Spectrum, Philadelphia, Pennsylvania, USA
27th April	Rensselaer Polytechnic Institute, Fieldhouse, New York, USA
28th April	Civic Centre, Providence, Rhode Island, USA
29th April	Civic Arena, Pittsburgh, Pennsylvania, USA
1st May	Rosemont Horizon, Chicago, Illinois, USA
2nd May	Market Square Arena, Indianapolis, Indiana, USA
4th May	Kiel Auditorium, St Louis, Missouri, USA
5th May	Kemper Arena, Kansas City, Missouri, USA
7th May	Wings Stadium, Kalamazoo, Michigan, USA
8th May	Joe Louis Arena, Detroit, Michigan, USA
9th May	Riverfront Coliseum, Cincinnati, Ohio, USA
11th May	The Coliseum, Richfield, Ohio, USA
13th May	Sports Arena, Toledo, Ohio, USA
15th May	Civic Arena, St Paul, Minnesota, USA
17th May	Alpine Valley Music Theatre, East Troy, Wisconsin, USA
22nd May	Irvine Meadows Amphitheatre, Los Angeles, California, USA
23rd May	Irvine Meadows Amphitheatre, Los Angeles, California, USA
24th May	Shoreline Amphitheatre, Mountain View, California, USA
27th May	Cal Expo Amphitheatre, Sacramento, California, USA
29th May	Sports Arena, San Diego, California, USA
30th May	Veterans Memorial Coliseum, Phoenix, Arizona, USA

*** Blackmore broke his finger during this concert.***
The following dates were then cancelled:

31st May	*Tingley Coliseum, Albuquerque, New Mexico, USA*
1st June	*Houston, Texas, USA*
-- June	*Dallas, Texas, USA*
5th June	*Tarrant County Convention Centre, Fort Worth, Texas, USA*
13th June	*The Omni, Atlanta, Georgia, USA*
15th June	*Sportatorium, Hollywood, Florida, USA*
20th June	*Coliseum, Nassau, New York, USA*
22nd June	*Meadowlands Arena, East Rutherford, New Jersey, USA*

Tour Dates

19th August	Jäähalli, Helsinki, Finland
22nd August	Valle Hovin Stadion, Oslo, Norway
26th August	Stadthalle, Vienna, Austria
27th August	Sporthalle, Linz, Austria
29th August	Messegelände, Nürnberg, Germany
30th August	F.C.P. Stadion, Pforzheim, Germany
31st August	Stadion am Riederwald, Frankfurt/Main, Germany
1st September	Palatrussardi, Milan, Italy *Rescheduled from 3rd September*
2nd September	Palatrussardi, Milan, Italy
5th September	Palazzo Della Civilta E Del Lavoro, Rome, La Paleur, Italy
6th September	Palazzo Della Civilta E Del Lavoro, Rome, La Paleur, Italy *Rescheduled from 4th September*
7th September	Arena di Verona, Verona, Italy

1988

13th July	Burg Frankenstein, Darmstadt, Germany
	Launch party for Nobody's Perfect
31st July	Piazzale di via Mazzini, Jesi, Italy
11th August	Hammerjacks, Baltimore, Maryland, USA

*** Warm-up show in a club prior to major gigs.***
All US dates bar one one were cancelled. Known cancellations are:

12th August	*Springfield, Massachusetts, USA*
13th August	*Civic Centre, Providence, Rhode Island, USA*
16th August	Giants Stadium, East Rutherford, New Jersey, USA
9th September	Campi di Bisenzio, Florence, Italy
10th September	Stadium Simonetti Lamberti, Cava de' Tirreni, Italy
13th September	Stadio Friuli, Udine, Italy
14th September	Festa de l'Unita, Modena, Italy
15th September	Palasport, Genova, Italy
17th September	Ippodromo, Merano, Italy
19th September	Civic Arena, Milan, Italy
20th September	Palaeur, Rome, Italy
21st September	Palasport, Torino, Italy
24th September	Eissporthalle, Kassel, Germany
25th September	Sporthalle, Köln, Germany
27th September	Valby Hallen, Copenhagen, Denmark
28th September	Sporthalle Hamburg, Germany
	Rescheduled from 27th September
29th September	Stadthalle 1, Bremen, Germany

1993

The twenty-fifth anniversary tour was due to start in North America, but all shows were cancelled. The official reason given was that the release date of The Battle Rages On... had to be put back to allow for it to be re-mixed, but the truth was more likely down to poor ticket sales.

Known cancelled gigs are as follows:

27th July	Binghamton, Broom County, New York, USA
28th July	Performance Arts Centre, Saratoga, New York, USA
30th July	Lake Centre Darien, New York, USA
31st July	Star Lake Amphitheatre, Pittsburgh, Pennsylvania, USA
1st August	Kingswood, Toronto, Ontario, Canada
3rd August	Le Colisee, Quebec City, Quebec, Canada
4th August	Forum, Montreal, Quebec, Canada
7th August	Jones Beach, Long Island, New York, USA
8th August	Thames River Music Centre, Groton, Connecticut, USA
10th August	Great Woods, Mansfield, Massachusetts, USA
11th August	Fairgrounds, Allentown, Pennsylvania, USA
13th August	Garden State, Holmdel, New Jersey, USA
14th August	Mann Centre, Philadelphia, Pennsylvania, USA
15th August	Marriweather, Washington, D.C., USA
17th August	Walnut Creek, Raleigh, North Carolina, USA
18th August	Carowinds, Charlotte, North Carolina, USA
20th August	Riverbend, Cincinnati, Ohio, USA
21st August	Alpine Valley, Troy, Michigan, USA
22nd August	Poplar Creek, Hoffman Estates, Illinois, USA
24th August	Blossom Music Centre, Cuyahoga Falls, Ohio, USA
25th August	Pine Knob Music Theatre, Clarkston, Michigan, USA
27th August	Deer Creek, Indianapolis, Indiana, USA
28th August	Riverport, St. Louis, Missouri, USA
29th August	Sandstone, Bonner Springs, Kansas, USA
21st September	Festspiel and Kongreßhaus, Bregenz, Austria
	Full dress rehearsal and filmed in part by MTV
24th September	Palaghiaccio, Rome, Italy
25th September	Palasport, Forli, Italy

Perfect Strangers - *Deep Purple 1984-1993*

26th September	Palatrussardi, Milan, Italy
27th September	Palasport, Torino, Italy
29th September	Stadthalle, Villach, Austria
1st October	Sporthalle, Schwerin, Germany
2nd October	Ostseehalle, Kiel, Germany
3rd October	Festhalle, Frankfurt/Main, Germany
4th October	Grugahalle, Essen, Germany
6th October	Weser-Ems-Halle, Oldenburg, Germany
7th October	Deutschlandhalle, Berlin, Germany
8th October	Sporthalle, Hamburg, Germany
10th October	Sporthalle, Köln, Germany
11th October	Eissporthalle, Memmingen, Germany
13th October	Frankenhalle, Nürnberg, Germany
14th October	Olympiahalle, München, Germany
15th October	Maimarkthalle, Mannheim, Germany
16th October	Hanns-Martin-Schleyer-Halle Stuttgart, Germany
18th October	Zenith, Nancy, France
19th October	Zenith, Paris, France
21st October	Hallenstadion, Zürich, Switzerland
22nd October	Patinoire de Malley, Prilly / Lausanne, Switzerland
26th October	Olympiahalle, Innsbruck, Austria
27th October	Stadthalle, Halle D, Vienna, Austria
29th October	Jubiläumshalle, Wels, Austria
30th October	Sportovny Hala, Prague, Czech Republic
31st October	Hala Widowiskowo-Sportowa, Zabrze, Poland
2nd November	Forest National, Brussels, Belgium
3rd November	Ahoy Sportpaleis, Rotterdam, Netherlands
5th November	Apollo, Manchester, England
7th November	Brixton Academy, London, England
8th November	Brixton Academy, London, England
9th November	NEC, Birmingham, England
12th November	Valby Hallen, Copenhagen, Denmark
13th November	Isstadion, Stockholm, Sweden
15th November	Spektrum, Oslo, Norway
17th November	Jäähalli, Helsinki, Finland